TEILHARD
AND THE
UNITY OF KNOWLEDGE

The Georgetown University Centennial Symposium
edited by

Thomas M. King, S.J.

&

James F. Salmon, S.J.

Paulist Press ◆ *New York/Ramsey*

Acknowledgement
The symposium that gave birth to this book, and the published volume itself, were funded in
part through a generous grant from the National Endowment for the Humanities.

Library of Congress
Catalog Card Number: 82-60590

ISBN: 0-8091-2491-2

Published by Paulist Press
545 Island Road, Ramsey, N.J. 07446

Printed and bound in the
United States of America

Contents

1

Introduction

Teilhardians had long known that May 1, 1981—the centennial of the birth of Pierre Teilhard de Chardin—had to be celebrated in a special way. Two Teilhardian Jesuits would be at Georgetown University on that date. One is a theologian who had long taught a course titled, Teilhard and Some Theologies of Evolution, and the other is a chemist who was about to teach Teilhard for the first time as part of an interdepartmental course titled, Issues in Science and Religion. We found that we had a similar appreciation of Teilhard. He had seemed to speak to us before we really understood what he was saying. We were particularly conscious of the diverse ways we had come to know: some of our knowledge had the objectivity of science, and some had the subjectivity of human relationships. Both of us had been formed by years of studying philosophy and a love of music. And we both had a sense that God is at the center of it all. Teilhard seemed to be speaking in terms of all of these sensitivities at the same time. In reading about him we seemed to better know ourselves and our significance as scholars. We wanted to tell others what Teilhard meant to us, so we chose an appropriate theme: Teilhard and the Unity of Knowledge.

In the Autumn of 1954 Teilhard was one of seventy scholars invited to a Symposium at Columbia University titled: The Unity of Knowledge. He was not one of the speakers, but his friend, Julian Huxley, spoke of him and told of Teilhard's understanding of the Noosphere, for the Noosphere involves a growing unification of knowledge. It is important to understand that Teilhard always distinguished between two forms of unity. One type would require that all things merge together to form a fusion of elements. The other would involve an organic unity wherein each individual difference would be heightened. It is this second type of unity that must constitute the Noosphere, and knowledge is of this second type. If our knowledge is true, it should give new sharpness to the data that is known; each detail should gain meaning through the universal statement. Teilhard envisioned the fields of knowledge coming together, but he saw them each retaining their own identity. To explain the Unity of Knowledge that we were seeking in our Symposium we used a quotation from the Introduction of THE PHENOMENON OF MAN:

> Like the meridians as they approach the poles, science, philosophy and religion are bound to converge as they draw nearer to the whole. I say "converge" advisedly, but without merging, and without ceasing, to the very end, to assail the real from different angles and on different planes.

By our Symposium we wanted to bring together significant scholars of our time in order that they might recall their common ideal of unity—lest their different methodologies draw them too far apart.

Plans for the Symposium were well underway when Stephen Jay Gould published an article accusing Teilhard of complicity in the famous Piltdown forgery of 1912. This charge appeared in the Natural History magazine for August 1980 and was quickly picked up by newspapers and more popular journals. Teilhard enthusiasts were stunned. We decided our Symposium could not ignore the charge and were glad to learn that J. S. Weiner was speaking in England in Teilhard's defense. J. S. Weiner—together with W. E. LeGros Clark and Kenneth Oakley—had uncovered the fraud in 1953. Even before the story broke in the press, Weiner went to Piltdown and tried to unravel the events that had taken place forty years before. In 1955 he published his conclusions with Oxford University Press as THE PILTDOWN FORGERY. Aware of the wealth of information that he had gathered and of the importance of his testimony, we wrote to Weiner and invited him to speak of Teilhard-Piltdown several days before the Symposium began. Dr. Weiner was happy to come. He stayed with us for a week and was a delight to all who came to know him. His talk on Teilhard-Piltdown is not included in this volume as it was not part of the Symposium and involved lengthy studies of the fossils with many maps and charts. As an appendix to this volume there is a brief response to Gould that includes numerous passages from the address that Weiner gave at Georgetown University on April 28, 1981.

For the Georgetown Symposium we had decided not to gather Teilhard experts to explore again his writings. Beyond the writings there is something else that could best be described as spirit. It is an adventuresome spirit that looks outward with openness and expectation. We began to consider adventuresome scholars who had gained recognition in their own fields. All of those whom we chose had expressed an interest in Teilhard. They each had done work in a field that is integral to the thought of Teilhard and each had thought in a global and evolutionary way. Those whom we asked seemed delighted to attend. One of them explained: "This year I had decided to turn down all speaking invitations. But this one I could not turn down."

Since we wanted the event to have a special character, we set a minimal charge of $10 for the weekend and $3 for students. This low charge meant that we had to look elsewhere for support. We made a request to the National Endowment for the Humanities, which was approved, and this approval more than anything else made the Symposium possible. The University made a contribution. The Jesuit Community at Georgetown opened its residence and dining room to speakers and respondents. The Symposium gained an international dimension when the French Embassy provided large photos of Teilhard and two films of his work. An Australian artist, Ray Reardon, came to exhibit his etchings done in the spirit of Teilhard. Since we wanted the speakers, respondents and general audience to interact we planned a reception for the opening night with cheese, champagne, and a large candle-covered ceremonial cake. Some local Teilhardians provided wine, flowers and baskets of fruit for the speakers' rooms. Both CBS and the Canadian Broadcasting Company came and made videotapes. CBS titled their program For Our Time, and the Canadian Broadcasting Company did a special film on the Teilhardian centennial. Student volunteers planned to act as ushers and parking lot attendants. Soon many of them were wearing red and gold T-shirts proclaiming the event.

On Friday, May 1—the last day of classes at Georgetown—more than the expected quota of things went wrong. It rained all day and traffic was tied up on Key Bridge. Workmen had left a barricade blocking one of the main entrances of the Healy Building. Paolo Soleri missed his plane in Indianopolis. Kenneth Boulding carried a large Teilhard display through the lobby of National Airport into the parking lot, only to find that the car sent for him would not start. But through these and many other difficulties a spirit of cooperation began to develop. People with long years of affection for Teilhard began to realize that there were hundreds who felt the same way. They shook rain from their coats and umbrellas, looked around and talked to strangers. The lighting added by the TV crew transformed Gaston Hall; a sense of expectation began to develop as though something different was about to happen. Beyond the intellectual adventure people had gathered to share, it seemed that a common spirit had drawn them together. It was the centennial date where one hundred years before there had been a specially graced moment. It seemed that another such moment was upon us. This Symposium would have the usual conflict of ideas and personalities. But beyond these all of those involved began to reach for something deeper.

At 7:40 P.M. Walter Burghardt, the moderator for the weekend, led Frederick Copleston and Ian Barbour to the stage of Gaston Hall. He welcomed those attending and announced that the Symposium would begin with a tape recording of the voice of Teilhard. This tape would have a brief passage that was recorded in 1948 at the Wenner Gren Foundation. Most of those attending had never seen or heard the man they had gathered to honor. The crowded auditorium quieted to hear a voice speaking in English with a heavy French accent:

> Each individual has something more because of his connection with other individuals. If you want a complete idea of man and of his evolution, you cannot find it in any individual. You would have to take two, or three, or five hundred human brains.

Seven hundred human brains had gathered at Georgetown University. They intensely felt their connection with each other. Soon they would reach for a more complete idea of themselves, their common evolution, and beyond this to their common destiny.

2

Teilhard de Chardin and a Global Outlook

Frederick C. Copleston, S.J.

In the letter of invitation which I received from the President of Georgetown University, the President stated that each speaker at this Symposium "will be asked to tell of his own work or research in a way that educated non-specialists can follow" and then relate what he has said "to other areas of knowledge or human concern," being mindful, in doing so, of Teilhard de Chardin. If therefore I begin this talk by referring to my own work, it is certainly not because I regard it as in any way comparable to the achievement of Teilhard de Chardin. I am simply carrying out the instructions given me by the President.

While I consider it a very great honor to be invited to give the opening talk at this Symposium, I feel a bit of a fraud. For I am far from being a specialist in Teilhardian studies, even though I included a section on his thoughts in the volume of my HISTORY OF PHILOSO-PHY which treats of French philosophy from the time of the revolution. As for Teilhard himself, I met him only once, in 1946, when I was taken to visit him by a Jesuit professor of theology at Lyons who later fell victim to Pope Pius XII's suspicions of what was sometimes called "The New Theology." Teilhard made a great impression on me, but at that time, of course, his famous writings had not yet been published. In later years, I have referred on a good many occasions to his thoughts as an example of the sort of overall interpretation of the world for which there is a real need. But I am not well acquainted with the details of his thought.

Turning to my own insignificant self—having been appointed in 1939 to lecture on the history of philosophy at the Jesuit center of theological and philosophical studies in England, I came to the conclusion that the available textbooks on this subject used in Catholic seminaries were inadequate. I decided to write one myself in three volumes, devoted respectively to ancient, medieval and modern philosophy. As some of you know, this work turned out to be much larger than I originally intended. It comprises nine volumes in hardback and seventeen in paperback. Nor is it finished, though it is most unlikely that I will ever complete it. In addition I have published a number of other works in the area of European philosophy, including volumes on St. Thomas Aquinas, Arthur Schopenhauer and Friedrich Nietzsche.

As time went on, I became more and more interested in certain general problems relating to the historical development of philosophical thought. For example, can we discern any recurrent patterns of thought in the philosophical traditions of different cultures? Again, are there any good reasons for supposing that the development of philosophical thought through the centuries exemplifies any laws? Further, as philosophical reflection is only one among the human being's cultural activities and is related to other factors in human life and culture, to what extent does honest reflection drive us in the direction of historical relativism? There are also, of course, problems relating to the objectivity of the history of philosophy, just as there are problems relating to historical objectivity in general. There are also problems relating to the criteria for assessing advance in philosophical thought.

In recent years I have published collections of essays in which I have dealt with some of these topics. But the projected large work has not seen the light of day. Nor is it likely to. For one thing, it very soon became clear to me that treatment of certain problems required a comparative study of the philosophical traditions of different cultures, and that what I could hope to achieve in this field was extremely limited. At the same time, even though I lack any knowledge of Eastern languages, I did not see why I should not make a modest contribution to the promotion of mutual understanding among peoples by discussing selected similarities and dissimilarities between the philosophies of different cultures. The result was a series of lectures given at Oxford in memory of Father Martin D'Arcy, which were published in 1980 by the Oxford University Press under the title *Philosophies and Cultures*. I continued this line of thought in my Gifford Lectures in the University of Aberdeen in the years 1979–1980.

Let me try to explain briefly what I mean, in the present context, by contributing to mutual understanding between peoples. It seems to me that it makes sense to talk about the different ways of thinking of different peoples. For example, philosophy in China, generally speaking, centered around the thought of the human being in a social context. There was metaphysics or cosmology in China, but the emphasis was laid on the human being as a moral agent in society. The official ideology in mainland China is now Marxism–Leninism, no longer Confucianism. Though, however, Marxism is a philosophy of Western origin, the change from the thought of imperial China to that of Communist China is not as great as the change would be from the traditional philosophy of India, which was predominantly one of liberation from this world, to the this-wordly Marxist system of thought. In other words, it seems to me that though individual systems of philosophy come and go, there can be ways of thought running through them which are more permanent. And if one can throw a little light on these basic different ways of thought, one is making some sort of contribution to mutual understanding among peoples, to intra-cultural dialogue. Obviously, what the philosopher can achieve in this respect is extremely limited. The fate of mankind depends on other factors besides what philosophers may say. This hardly needs saying. But it is not a good reason for doing nothing at all to promote intra-cultural dialogue and understanding, even if what one achieves is, at best, only a trifle.

In any case, in a world in which, in a real sense, we all stand or fall together, in which our fates and the fates of people in distant countries are inter-dependent, it seems to me highly desirable to transcend parochial attitudes and prejudices and to take a global view, a view of the human world as a whole. Just as there can be narrow attitudes in politics and a chauvinistic nationalism which despises or fails to understand and appreciate other nations and their problems, so can there be narrow-minded attitudes in philosophy, marked by a willed ignorance of or contempt for traditions other than one's own. An attempt to understand and appreciate the philosophical traditions of other cultures helps to overcome such narrow-minded attitudes and to achieve a more global consciousness. As an ancient Stoic might say, we are all citizens of the world.

What I have called a global consciousness is conspicuously exemplified in the thoughts of Teilhard de Chardin. I do not mean to imply that he was an expert in the history of philosophy, whether Western or Eastern. He was not. But he was acutely aware of the world as a whole, of the human race as a whole, and of our common vocation. It is sometimes said that the Frenchman is inclined to think that French culture is the only culture which really counts, and that though they are much less aggressive than, some other nations, the French tend to look on all other cultures as inferior to their own. I dare say that this sort of attitude is not confined to the French. In fact, it is not so confined. But at any rate, Teilhard de Chardin rose above any such parochial and limited outlook. And I feel ashamed of the fact that it is only in relatively advanced years that I have really come to feel the need for what I have called a global consciousness.

Turning to a rather different line of thought—on various occasions I have written and spoken against positivism and in favor of metaphysics. A good many years ago a reviewer of some book of mine said that my philosophizing seemed to consist in a perpetual dialogue with Professor A. J. Ayer, prolonging, as it were, my 1949 radio debate with him about logical positivism. I think, however, that this is a mistaken way of expressing the matter. To be sure, Ayer was the principal and best known representative of logical positivism in Great Britain, though he has modified some of his views in the course of time. But in spite of our radio discussion I did not think simply in terms of a debate with a particular philosopher, however eminent. As I now realize, the debate has been to a certain extent within myself. On the one hand, as I do not live and think in a state of isolation from all modern thought, I am conscious in myself of inclinations to believe that speculative metaphysics is pretty well devoid of cognitive value, and that empirical science is the only way of increasing our positive knowledge of reality. On the other hand, I am convinced that metaphysics has functions which cannot be performed by the empirical sciences. And I have argued in this sense, in spite of the uneasy feeling that some of the things which I have said are vulnerable to criticism and possibly fanciful. Hence it is not simply a case of Copleston versus Ayer. It is also a question of Copleston versus Copleston. Anyway, I would like to mention one particular line of thought in support of metaphysics. There is nothing new in it, I regret to say; but it is relevant in the present context.

It is unlikely that anyone will dispute the claim that analysis and synthesis are essential features of intellectual activity. To condemn analysis in the name of synthesis would be as absurd as to condemn synthesis in the name of analysis. Both are legitimate functions of the human mind. But at one time analysis may predominate, at another time synthesis. We can see this in the history of philosophy. In the construction of what are called world-views, overall interpretations of reality as known by us, the activity of synthesis has been conspicuous. In some other lines of thought, in certain currents of thought in the late Middle Ages, in the philosophizing of David Hume, and in the modern analytic movement, the critical and analytic activities of the human mind have been predominant. In my opinion, this ebb and flow of synthesis and analysis is not a phenomenon which should cause any surprise. It is what we might expect.

That the activity of analysis has a part to play in empirical science hardly needs saying. There is chemical analysis, for example. But the feature of empirical science to which I wish to draw attention and which can be associated with analysis is the proliferation of disciplines and subdisciplines. Ever since Hume's dream of the development of a science of the human being began to be fulfilled seriously the relevant sciences have tended to multiply. For example, we do not have simply psychology: we have child psychology, clinical psychology, educational psychology, industrial psychology, physiological psychology and social psychology. We do not have simply anthropology: we have, for instance, physical, cultural and social anthropology. Within any group of disciplines there can of course be overlapping and common features; but the need for specialization has entailed a proliferation of more or less distinct disciplines or subdisciplines. The same sort of thing can be found in physical or natural science. The general pattern seems to be that when a new science develops, biology for example, it tends to give birth to a plurality of subdisciplines.

This fragmentation of science has sometimes been regarded as something to be overcome. The members of the Vienna Circle and those associated with it hoped to be able to achieve a unification of the sciences through the construction of a common language. The enterprise can hardly be looked upon as ending in success. Quite apart, however, from the questionable program sponsored by the Vienna Circle, it is clear enough that science (I am thinking principally of physics) pursues not only an analytic but also a synthesizing activity. We have only to think of the way in which science coordinates phenomena under laws, more particular laws under more general laws, laws under theories. The limiting ideal would be, I suppose, to formulate certain most general and basic laws, from which all more particular laws in theoretical physics could be derived.

So far, so good. In view, however, of its evident synthesizing activity it may seem that science has been progressively taking over the activity of synthesis previously attributed to philosophy. Some of the outstanding philosophers, Spinoza for example, have had the vision of one intelligible universe. The people who have contributed to fulfilling the vision have been the outstanding scientists. This view of the matter can be expressed in a very plausible manner. It does not include dismissing metaphysics as nonsense. It simply claims that science is the heir of metaphysics in regard to its synthesizing function, provided at any rate that the word "science" is understood as covering not only natural sciences but also the sciences related, in various ways, to the human being. It is not a question of calling metaphysics "meaningless," nor of denying that it had any useful role to play in its time. It is a matter of arguing that the method or methods of empirical science are superior to the method of metaphysics in attaining positive knowledge of the world in which we live and act and of human beings themselves.

When people talk in this way, they generally assume that to all intents and purposes metaphysics can be identified with world-views, *Weltanschauungen*. This identification is doubtlessly open to challenge. But I do not wish to get involved in a discussion of what metaphysics is or ought to be. So let us agree to confine our attention to world-views.

In the first place the activity of synthesis which is exemplified in the attempt to construct a world-view seems to me a natural activity and one that fulfills a real need. Human beings find themselves in a world in which they live and act. It is natural that human beings should desire to obtain an overall view of their environment, physical and social, of their place in it, and of the meaning, if any, of human history. Obviously, most people have neither the time nor the inclination nor, in many cases, the ability to develop any systematic interpretation of the world in which they find themselves and in which they have to act. But at some time in their lives many people ask themselves, even if only fleetingly, a question such as "what is it all about?" or "is there any point to it?" They may of course dismiss such questions as unanswerable. But the raising of the questions expresses a need, a need which is natural enough.

In the second place I have no hesitation in saying that empirical science, in spite of its own synthesizing activity, cannot fulfill this need. Empirical science has indeed extended its scope to include the human being and human society. But it can do so only by objectifying man, by treating him as an object in the world, an object which can be investigated from the outside, as it were. But there is also the human being as subject, not simply as epistemological subject but also as the agent, who acts in the light of goals, for the attainment of ends, who evaluates in terms of good and evil, who can be dissatisfied with the actual and attempt to change it, who is open to the idea of a reality beyond this world, not identifiable with it. In other words, there is room for a synthesis in which the attempt is made to construct an overall harmonious view of reality, of the scientific conception of the world, of the human being's moral life, with its evaluation and ideals, of man's aesthetic experience and of his religious experience. As scientific activity and the scientific conception of the world constitute elements, though important elements of course, of the material which needs to be synthesized, to be brought together in one overall world-view, science obviously cannot itself fulfill this need.

The same point can be made by referring to the Wittgensteinian theory of language-games. Let us assume that it makes sense to talk about the language of science, the language of morals, religious language, and so on.[1] According to Wittgenstein each language-game expresses a "form of life." But even if this is the case, each form of life is a form of human life; and each language is a form of human language. All are related to human nature. It is natural to seek an overall view which will enable us to see similarities, dissimilarities and interrelations. But if the language of science constitutes only one of the factors which have to be taken into account in the development of an overall view, it cannot, by itself, provide the overall view.

It is hardly necessary to say that by an overall view I do not mean something analogous to an aerial photograph, in which particular details, as particulars, are included. What I have in mind is more or less what A. N. Whitehead had in mind when he defined speculative philosophy as "an endeavor to frame a coherent, logical, necessary system of ideas, in terms of which every element of an experience can be interpreted."[2] The need for such an overall synthesis has been felt by a number of philosophers, Kant for example. And it has not disappeared. In a novel by William Golding, FREE FALL, reference is made to two worlds, the scientific world and the ethico-religious world. The assertion is then made by one of the characters in the novel that while both worlds are real, there is no bridge between them. In my opinion, it is one of the tasks of philosophical thought to look for a "bridge," to attempt a synthesis, in which of course the component elements are not confused. I do not mean that all philosophers should undertake this task. Philosophers, like other people, have their own particular talents, inclinations, interests. If a philosopher is specially interested in, say, meta-ethics, it would be absurd to demand that he should set about constructing a world-view. What I claim is simply that there is a natural and obvious need for metaphysical synthesis and that this is a perfectly reasonable philosophical activity.

It can of course be objected that world-views succeed one another, and that this fact throws their cognitive value into question. But I do not wish to enter upon a discussion of this matter here. All that I can say now is this. If one understands by a world-view a system of necessarily true propositions or of basic categories which must be exemplified in any conceivable world, and if such a system is possible, then of course there can be a perennially true philosophical system. If, however, one understands a world-view to mean a synthesis which presupposes and takes as its point of departure contemporary science, for example, and contemporary social structures (and this, I think, is what is ordinarily meant by the term "world-view"), no world-view can be final and definitive, inasmuch as the substructure is subject to change. Hence fresh attempts at synthesis will be required.

Among recent attempts to meet the need to which I have referred, at any rate as far as science and religion are concerned, that of Teilhard de Chardin has been, for a good many minds, the most impressive. It is sometimes said that the so-called conflict between science and religion is a thing of the past. And for those of us who are not fundamentalists this may well be true as far as contradictions between certain scientific hypotheses and certain Biblical statements are concerned. If one does not look on the Bible as a scientific textbook or regard it as a source of scientific knowledge, apparent contradictions between science and the Scriptures can be resolved. Further, if a religion includes no factual statements about reality, about what exists, there can hardly be any formal clash between that religion and science. But a religion such as

Christianity (unless we pursue a policy of drastic reductionism) certainly does include beliefs about reality, about what is. The relevant religious statements can doubtless coexist with the statements of science, in the sense that they may be logically compatible. If any apparent logical incompatibility is discerned, it can be resolved either by an appropriate interpretation of the relevant religious statement or by distinguishing between more or less established scientific knowledge and questionable hypotheses or theories proposed by scientists. But the coexistence of a set of scientific statements and a set of religious beliefs about reality is not enough to satisfy the reflective mind. For one thing, it is the human being who pursues scientific inquiry, and it is the human being who believes religious doctrines. It is natural to look for some closer relation between the two than that of coexistence. For another thing, it seems to a good many people that while scientific statements are subject to falsification or confirmation, directly or indirectly, what the religious believer regards as truths of faith transcend the ordinary criteria for assessing truth or falsity. It may therefore seem that even if science and religious belief can coexist, the former, in its development and advance, is destined to drive out the latter, as far, that is to say, as religious beliefs about reality, about what is the case, are concerned. Teilhard, however, tried to show how science and religion converge together in one total vision as the world. For him, it was not simply a case of coexistence but rather of interpenetration. It seems to me safe to say that it was this overall vision which chiefly impressed many of his readers.

Vision may be a vague word, but I use it deliberately. If we start scrutinizing the details of Teilhard's world-view and ask for argument or proof, all sorts of objections come to mind, objections on the score of lack of clarity and precision of thought, objections from the side of science (for example, that on the basis of a particular scientific theory an edifice is constructed, the weight of which the hypothesis cannot bear), objections from a philosophical point of view (for example, that the construction is a mixture of science, metaphysics, poetry and personal religious faith), objections from the side of theology (for example, that there is a marked tendency to divinize the world, that redemption comes through Christ crucified and risen and not through "matters" actualization of its potentialities,[3] and that Teilhard's optimistic account of the world-process not only pays far too little attention to the dark side of human life and history but also receives little support from the Gospels). To those, however, who feel the persuasive force of the vision as a whole, objection made by scientists, professional philosophers and the theologians are apt to seem pedantic, captious and carping. Such people would probably agree with the Russian religious thinker, Nikolai Berdyaev that "what carries conviction is not discursive argument but the original insight."[4] In Berdyaev's opinion, the impact of the philosophical tradition from Parmenides to Hegel is "to freeze cold everything it touches".[5] However this may be, one could hardly claim that Teilhard's world-vision has this particular effect.

To avoid any possible misunderstanding, I had better make it clear that I value clarity and precision of thought, that I do not think that all objections against Teilhard's thought can be dismissed as captious, and that I have no wish to reduce philosophy to expressions of highly personal visions of the universe. Though one can certainly feel on occasion that what one says is an inadequate expression of what one wishes to say, I would not care to assert with Berdyaev that though thought must be expressed, it becomes a lie once it has been expressed.[6] At the same time there is such a thing as "vision," and it can play an important role even in metaphysical thought. For example, in the case of Spinoza the general idea of the universe as a totality, as the one ultimate reality, doubtless preceded, not followed, the claims of arguments presented in his *Ethics*. To be sure, the initial general idea which presumably seemed to Spinoza to express an insight or vision became a philosophical system only when it had been made explicit and developed by reasoning. But it by no means follows that Spinoza came to believe in *Natura seu Deus* only as a result of his own arguments as presented in the *Ethics*. The general idea or global vision came first. Similarly, Teilhard's thinking as presented in the relevant works was doubtless the explicitation of a general vision of the world, a vision in which science and religion were not left in a state of tension, nor simply as coexisting but unrelated entities, but were fused in one whole.

By using words such as "vision" and "insight" I do not intend to imply that the relevant general or global idea is self-authenticating or unquestionable, even if it may appear in this light to the philosopher himself. It may be open to criticism, on the ground that it is partial, for example, the result of focusing attention on one aspect of the world to the exclusion of another. Nor of course is its explicitation in discursive reasoning immune from critical analysis. Nor are the arguments which purport to support truth-claims made on its behalf. At the same time the persuasive force of a philosophical world-view depends very much on the qualities of the general vision which it exhibits. If it seems to people to be the sort of thing which they were looking for, to solve tensions, perplexities, problems in their own minds, to fit in with their experience and at the same time to enrich it, they are disposed to accept it, at any rate in outline. And they are more induced to look for answers to objections than to assent easily to the objections. I have no doubt that this has been the case with a good many people in regard to Teilhard de Chardin. He offers them a contemporary world-view which seems to enable them not simply to believe in but also to see an interpenetration of the spheres of science and religion and so to overcome the uneasy feeling that science does not so much contradict religious belief as render it more and more irrelevant. Some would claim that however impressive Teilhard's world-view may seem at first sight, it falls to pieces when subjected to critical analysis. But it was a real problem which Teilhard tackled, and a real need which he tried to meet. There is a place for metaphysical vision, and I do not myself think that his world-vision must entirely fall to pieces or dissolve under the impact of critical analysis.

In the foregoing remarks I have several times used the general word "religion." But Teilhard, as we all know, was concerned not so much with religion in general as with Christianity in particular. From one point of view his thought can be seen as a form of Christian apologetics. And I wish to make a few observations about this aspect of his activity. What seems to me to have been his basic problem is one which can occur, and frequently does occur even to the minds of a good many reflective Christian believers. And I, at any rate, have a good deal of sympathy with the way in which he tackled it. I admit, however, that the way in which he tackled it gives rise to questions, in my mind at any rate, to which I cannot give satisfactory answers.

It is hardly necessary to say that today our knowledge of other cultures is far greater than that possessed by medieval Christendom. And that Christianity should tend to appear as being simply one among the so-called world-religions is natural enough. For, from the empirical point of view, this is what it is. Christ seems to many minds to be simply one of the great religious teachers who have appeared in the history of mankind. And it can easily seem that the expansive religions have entered into a state of more or less peaceful coexistence, confronting together a growing secularist movement. At the same time Christianity has not renounced its claim to universality. Orthodox Christians still believe that Christ is the redeemer and savior of all mankind, the mediator, in a unique sense, between God and the human being, and that the

Church has a divinely-given universal mission. The question arises therefore whether the truth of this claim is really credible. Is it something to which Christians simply pay lip-service, while they do not really believe it? Is not the Church too weighed down by thought-forms and structures from the past that it cannot reasonably be expected to be the center of devotion for all mankind? In fine, is not the Christian religion too parochial, too tied to certain cultural traditions, for its claim to universality to be really credible?

Teilhard de Chardin was evidently acutely aware of this sort of problem. He had been brought up in a devout Catholic family, and he retained his faith. But his intellectual development and his experiences were such that he could not fail to be aware of such problems; and I assume that he felt their impact within himself. In tackling the problems, he did not have recourse to the kind of arguments which one can find in the old-fashioned textbooks of apologetics. Nor did he emphasize the line of thought represented so ably by Maurice Blondel. He presented a world-view in which the risen Christ appeared in the center of the picture, so to speak, the cosmic Christ, and in which the process of cosmogenesis, in the extrapolated theory of evolution, appeared as a process of Christogenesis, the birth and development of the total Christ, Christ in his mystical body. Cosmological and Christian conceptions of the world converge in Teilhard's thought. He tries not so much to convince people by abstract arguments as to make them "see" the relevance of Christianity, the universal role or function of Christ in a world which manifests the creative activity of God. In other words, he provides a global vision which makes Christianity's claim to universality more credible. It can reasonably be argued that this is what people need, namely a vision, and that they are more likely to be favorably impressed by a contemporary vision which widens their mental horizons than by the stock arguments of traditional apologetics.

As we have already recalled, among the objections which have been brought against Teilhard's thought some have been of a theological character. I am not concerned here with examining and discussing any particular objections of this sort. I would like to point out, however, that Teilhard was what we might perhaps describe as an experimental thinker. What I mean by this is that he did not content himself with repeating what others had said before him. He thought that a fresh Christian vision of the world was required, and he tried to supply one, one which could impress the minds of those who were otherwise inclined to look on the Christian religion as played out, as having no message of value for modern man or as being pretty well irrelevant in the context of modern science and thought and of man's striving after the realization of ideals in this world. We can say, I suppose, that Teilhard wished to overcome the bifurcation between the supernatural and the natural, bifurcation which can have the result either that belief in the supernatural is jettisoned in favor of an affirmation of the natural or that the natural, God's creation, is belittled or despised in comparison with the supernatural. For the conception of a bifurcated reality, a conception which tended to produce world-fleeing or world-despising supernaturalists on the one hand and materialists, naturalists and positivists on the other, he wished to substitute a unified conception of reality, a Christocentric conception in which the Christian element, so to speak, would be not an addition, something added on to a non-Christian or a neutral picture of the world, but an integrating factor in the total world-view. In the process of experimentation, in trying to develop a fresh vision, he not unnaturally expounded views or made statements which some theologians and ecclesiastics would find it difficult to reconcile with their standards of orthodoxy. But it is hard to see how we can have things both ways. On the one hand we can try to prevent creative and original thought, to disallow it as dangerous. On the other hand we can allow it, even encourage it, with the awareness that some odd-sounding statements are likely to be made or questionable ideas tried out. But we can hardly pursue both policies at the same time.

Teilhard was not and did not claim to be a professional theologian. But there is a somewhat analogous situation in the theological area. The Church encourages professional theologians to attempt the restatement of Christian doctrine in terms which the minds of people today can more easily understand and to exhibit in fresh ways the relevance of these doctrines to Christian life. Theologians cannot do this without experiments in thought. They must therefore be free to experiment, unless creative theological thought is to be stifled.[7]

What I have said in this talk may have given the impression to some hearers that I am a Teilhardian, an enthusaistic adherent and worshipper at the shrine. This is not the case. If I have abstained almost entirely from criticism, this is not because I see nothing in his thought to criticize, but because I wished to dwell on some positive aspects. It seems to me that there is certainly a need for a fresh Christian vision of the world and for a re-thinking, from within Christianity, of the world-wide significance and relevance of the Christian faith. I honor and respect Teilhard de Chardin for his impressive attempt to meet this need.

As I have said, we need creative thinkers. And Teilhard was one of them. He was a Christian thinker. Sir Julian Huxley, a friend and admirer of Teilhard, felt himself unable to accept the Christian element in Teilhard's vision of the world. But for Teilhard himself the Christian element was not an optional addition, so to speak, but an integral part of the vision. His world-view centered around the risen Christ, who was not on the periphery but in the center. Whether the scientific hypothesis of evolution can legitimately be stretched and extended in the way in which Teilhard (and to a certain extent Huxley himself) extended it is open to discussion. Questions have also been asked about the relation between the cosmic Christ and the Jesus of the Gospels. Teilhard might reply that the concept of the cosmic Christ can be found in the epistles of St. Paul and in the Apocalypse, though not, of course, in the context of the modern theory of evolution. In any case, Teilhard did not claim to have presented us with the complete truth in its final and definitive form. He tried to get us to "see" something, to share his general vision of reality as a framework for life. And we can certainly pay honor to him as an outstanding and inspiring visionary and religious thinker of our times.

NOTES

1. By "language-games" Wittgenstein seems to have meant primarily linguistic operations such as asserting, commanding, questioning, and so on. But the interpretation in terms of the language of science, the language of morals and so on is not without foundation in the writings of Wittgenstein himself.

2. *Process and Reality,* p. 4.

3. Teilhard did not, of course, claim that salvation comes from self-actualizing matter, nor, indeed, that "matter" actualizes itself, as the sole cause of the process of evolution. But the impression has sometimes been formed that he did think in this way.

4. *Dream and Reality, An Essay in Autobiography,* translated by K. Lampert, p. 81 (London, 1950).

5. *Ibid.,* p. 287.

6. *Ibid.,* p. 285. Berdyaev quotes Tyutchev (in the latter's poem *Silentium*).

7. I am talking here about the restatement of doctrine, involving a process of re-conceptualization, not about denying defined doctrines or jettisoning essential portions of the Christian faith. That is, I am talking about creative thought within Christianity, not about pursuing a policy which can reasonably be regarded as putting the thinker outside the Christian religion.

SUMMARY OF RESPONSE AND DISCUSSION

Frederick Copleston's talk was followed by a response from Ian Barbour. Dr. Barbour's father had worked extensively with Teilhard and Dr. Barbour had known Teilhard in both China and New York. He began by telling of Teilhard's kindness and added that the intensity of his religious commitment was evident to all who knew him. Copleston had compared Teilhard with Whitehead and Barbour developed this comparison:

> Our theme at this conference is the unity of knowledge. I would suggest that both Teilhard and Whitehead were driven to seek this unity partly out of concern for intellectual coherence and a search for universal metaphysical categories which were applicable to all aspects of experience. This is the metaphysician's quest. In both men there was the strong sense of the continuity of reality—both the continuity of evolutionary history and the continuity of gradations among levels of reality in the present. For both, the coherence of the world was ultimately the product of the unified purpose of God.

Barbour went on to speak of Teilhard's evolutionary and cosmic perspective leading him "to reformulate and reconceptualize the traditional western concept of God in ways that may be more universal."

In his talk Copleston had warned lest Christian faith be linked with any scientific hypothesis that may be later discarded. Barbour expressed some reservation; he allowed that the details of evolutionary theory may be modified, but "the picture of nature as a dynamic, changing, interdependent process is here to stay." Dr. Bernard Towers intervened from the floor to say that for Teilhard, for himself and many others, evolution is in no sense a hypothesis. Copleston responded that today most logicians term all empirical statements as hypotheses.

19

This does not mean that they are not well founded. If I spoke of evolution as a scientific hypothesis, I simply meant that it was an informative statement about the world that was not contradictory to deny.—Not that we have any good evidence to deny it.

A final intervention from the floor offered a different perspective: "Teilhard sensed Christ coming into being in the world. If that basic intuition is applied to biology, you come up with the theory of evolution whether you intended it or not."

3

Time and the Unity of Knowledge

Ilya Prigogine

I

It is quite a privilege to be associated with this celebration of Teilhard de Chardin. The work he has left has so many aspects that it can be a focus of interest for a wide variety of people including scientists, philosophers and historians. Let me first try to situate the problematic of Teilhard. I believe that the nineteenth century left us with a conflictive situation. On the one side it was a period of unprecedented growth of western science with its emphasis on a time-independent objective description of nature. As beautifully expressed by Berlin in his book AGAINST THE CURRENT:

> They sought all-embracing schemas, universal unifying frameworks, within which everything that exists could be shown to be systematically—i.e., logically or causally—interconnected, vast structures in which there should be no gaps left open for spontaneous, unattended developments, where everything that occurs should be, at least in principle, wholly explicable in terms of immutable general laws.[1]

This ideal of science to reach an unchanging, eternal reality was expressed again and again by the greatest mathematicians and physicists of the 19th century. The aim of scientific description was to reduce nature to the laws of motion as established once and for all by Newton. And as is well known, future and past play identical roles in the laws of motion. The basic equation of Newton relating acceleration to force remains invariant when you replace time t by $-t$, that is, if we exchange future and past.

One of the main fascinations of modern science was precisely the feeling that science had exorcised time, that it could be formulated entirely in terms of basic eternal laws in which no reference to time need ever be made. This gave us a feeling of intellectual security, which was expressed with great clarity by the French sociologist Lévy-Bruhl, who has written:

> Our feeling of intellectual security is so deeply anchored in us that we even do not see how it could be shaken. Suppose even that we would observe some phenomenon seemingly quite mysterious; we still would remain persuaded that our ignorance is only provisional, that this phenomenon must satisfy the general laws of causality, and that the reasons for which it has appeared will be determined sooner or later. *The nature which surrounds us is order and reason, exactly as is the human mind.* Our everyday activity implies a perfect confidence in the universality of the laws of nature.[2]

This rejection of time has introduced into Western culture a rift, a duality which we begin only now to overcome. After all, time is the fundamental experience of man. The impossibility to escape time, the notions of destiny, the consciousness of death, have always been the main sources of inspiration for literature and art. It is not astonishing that an atemporal science has led to what Lenoble has called "the anxiety of modern man."

Must science be defined in terms of ruptures between man and nature? Is this really true, as Monod has stated:

> Man must at last wake out of his millenary dream; and in doing so, wake to his total solitude, his fundamental isolation. Now does he at last realize that, like a gypsy, he lives on the boundary of an alien world. A world that is deaf to his music, just as indifferent to his hopes as it is to his suffering or his crimes.[3]

It is interesting that the problem of time dominates the birth of modernity at the very start of the twentieth century, in science and in philosophy. It plays a crucial role both in the work of Einstein and of Bergson. It seems interesting in the present context to contrast their positions with that of Teilhard.

Einstein starts with subjective time as perceived by each of us, but time acquires an objective meaning only when it can be measured and communicated from one observer to another.[4] A large part of Einstein's creative work deals with this problem of the communication of time between observers occupying different situations, and in different gravitational fields one with respect to the other. And as you know, Einstein found that time is dependent on the physical conditions in which the observer is; it is sensitive to gravitational fields. This work led Einstein to some of the most striking discoveries ever made, such as the fact that the gravitational field slows down the motion of clocks.

And it is curious that this inquiry about the communication of time led to the discovery that in some circumstances this communication is impossible. For example, there can be no communication of time between a hypothetical observer sitting on one of the famous black holes and an observer at a safe distance from its intense gravitational field. The problem of subjective time, with its essential distinction between the future, the present, and the past, did not escape Einstein, but it seemed to him to be outside science. In the recollections of Carnap we may read the following:

Once Einstein said that the problem of the Now worried him seriously. He explained that the experience of the Now means something special for man, something essentially different from the past and the future, but that this important difference does not and cannot occur within physics. That this experience cannot be grasped by science seemed to him a matter of painful but inevitable resignation. I remarked that all that occurs objectively can be described in science; on the one hand the temporal sequence of events is described in physics; and, on the other hand, the peculiarities of man's experiences with respect to time, including his different attitude towards past, present, and future, can be described and (in principle) explained in psychology. But Einstein thought that these scientific descriptions cannot possibly satisfy our human needs;

that there is something essential about the Now which is just outside of the realm of science.[5]

This is a dualistic conclusion: the time of science as opposed to an internal "non-scientific" time.

It is interesting that Bergson, following in a sense an opposite road, reaches also a dualistic conclusion. Bergson also starts with a subjective time and then studies its objectivization through physics. However, for him, this objectivization leads to an impoverishment of time. Internal existential time has qualitative features which are lost in this process. It is for this reason Bergson introduces the distinction between time and duration and develops a world view, one can say, based on this duality.

Such dualistic conclusions could not satisfy Teilhard. His whole conception expresses a deep drive towards unity. Again and again he speaks of the "nostalgie de l'unité," of the necessity not to oppose matter, life or men but to see all manifestations of nature as united by the concept of time, of evolution. It is true that there is a curious duality in Teilhard's approach. Probably his contribution having the largest scientific component is his LE PHENOMENE HUMAIN.[6] Everybody knows the famous preface in which he asks that one should read this book only and exclusively as a scientific memoir: "It deals with man solely as a phenomenon; but it also deals with the whole phenomenon of man." I find the use of the word "phenomene" quite characteristic of the approach of Teilhard. His description of evolution is basically phenomenological, one could nearly say positivistic. He tries to describe evolution as it may have been without, in fact, dealing with any question concerning the mechanism of this evolution. He is satisfied to note that there must be some explanation for the transition from non-life to life, but he is satisfied with a few short, and we may even say a little naive, remarks concerning the mechanism of this transition. In many of his writings, he comes back to this problem of the mechanism of complexification, but it is more the fact of this complexification than its mechanism which is obviously his main interest. It seems to me not unjust to state that in Teilhard's work we find a phenomenological descriptive vision of the past together with a lyrical prophetic vision of the future. These two parts are unified by a concept of a polarized time with an infinite, evolutionary potential.

What can be our appreciation of Teilhard's work a little more than twenty-five years after his death? I think it has to be recognized that this role of time, of evolution, the concept of an historical world, has become more and more prevalent on all levels of science, from elementary particles up to the cosmological scale. This is indeed a deep change, so deep that I believe that we are living through one of the greatest revolutions in Western science since its very formulation by Newton. At the dawn of modern science, the Milesian school, of which Thales was one of the most illustrious proponents, introduced the idea of a primordial matter closely related to the concept of conservation of matter. For Thales, a single substance (such as water) forms the primordial matter; all changes in physical phenomena, such as growth and decay, must therefore be mere illusions. We have to look for the stable element in the changing universe. You all know how beautifully Lucretius expressed that we have to look for the hidden behind the obvious:

Still, lest you happen to mistrust my words
because the eye cannot perceive prime bodies
hear now of particles you must admit
exist in the world and yet cannot be seen.[7]

During the two thousand years or so since Lucretius wrote the *De Natura Rerum,* these particles have gone through a lot of changes. They became molecules, atoms, elementary particles; but the idea of a close association between reality and some permanent elements has dominated Western thought throughout.

Today there is a deep change going on, which I myself have experienced over the period I have been interested in science. When I started my work, few people were interested in the problem of time, of evolution, of complexification. But today there is an enormous effort going on with these questions in mind. And as I shall try to show in this lecture, the role of time leads to an increased unity between the various sciences, physics, chemistry, and biology. Moreover, they contribute to remove the dualism we noticed at the start of this lecture. Time does not oppose us to the universe; perhaps more so, we could say it expresses our participation in an evolving universe. In this context, science is defined less in terms of ruptures than in terms of participation of man in the universe he describes. It is certainly a remarkable coincidence that this evolution of science proceeds in the middle of the explosive growth of human society, which will affect the relation between man and man, man and nature. This coincidence exemplifies the unity of science and culture. It is well in line with the global view taken by Teilhard according to which evolution has to affect all levels of the existence of man.

II

I would like to briefly retrace how time, oriented time, appeared more and more clearly as a factor in physics and chemistry. Historical time was once thought to be reserved for sciences dealing with biological, social and cultural phenomena but the strange story of the dialogue between man and nature, full of dramatic incidents, has led us to realize the importance of historical time even in physics and chemistry. The idea of nature as atoms and the void, which can be described by Newtonian physics, was thought by many to be permanently established. But the pressure of new discoveries and new ideas has forced us to write a new and fascinating chapter of the dialogue between man and nature which could be described as going from the concept of being in a static sense to the concept of being as becoming.

Modern science starts with Newton's synthesis and its description of motion in terms of trajectories. As I have noted no distinction appears between future and past. Moreover, a motion in one direction can go as well in another direction. However, our everyday experience shows that most phenomena which occur around us cannot satisfy laws in which past and future play the same role. Time displays an obvious one-sidedness and direction. For example, if we heat part of a macroscopic body like a piece of iron and then isolate this body thermally, we observe that the temperature of the piece of iron becomes uniform over a period of time. The second law of thermodynamics was formulated during the nineteenth century to summarize the characteristic features of such a process. This law introduced a function, a concept, called entropy, which makes a distinction between what are called reversible and irreversible processes. In Figure 1 we see a schematic formulation of the law for open physical systems.

There is entropy which can transfer across the boundaries of the system, call it d_eS, and an entropy production within the system, call it d_iS. The formulation of the second law says that this latter entropy production, d_iS, is positive because of the existence of irreversible processes in nature; like the example of the temperature of the piece of iron becoming uniform over a period of time.[8] All kinds of transformations

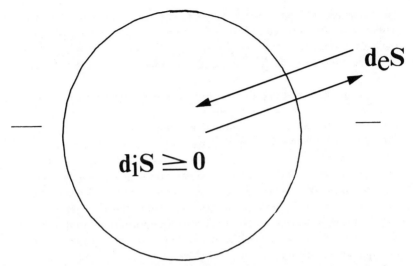

Figure 1. *Open Systems:* Internal entropy production $d_iS \geq 0$. d_eS is the exchange of entropy with the environment.

such as chemical reactions and heat flow are irreversible processes. The important point is that they are one-sided, in that the future does not play the same role as the past.

It is interesting to broadly separate the history of thermodynamics into three stages. In the first part of the nineteenth century people considered the conditions under which the entropy production vanished, that is d_iS goes to zero, which permitted the study and understanding of an enormous variety of physical phenomena; for example, phase transitions like the melting of ice to water. This first stage is the world of equilibrium. Then in the middle of the century the development of linear thermodynamics took place which was concerned with near-equilibrium conditions. In this world a system remains stable despite small perturbations or fluctuations. For example, slight changes in concentrations of some reactants at constant temperature and volume cause small fluctuations, but damping mechanisms can set in among large populations of molecules which bring the system back to the equilibrium state. More recently a third stage has occurred in which large deviations from equilibrium have been studied. This far-from-equilibrium condition produces surprising features not found in the equilibrium and near-equilibrium worlds. We find that small fluctuations or perturbations may drive a system under certain conditions towards new structures which are quite unexpected from classical views of chemistry. Thus the worlds of equilibrium and near-equilibrium are stable worlds, but the situation changes completely when we go to a far-from-equilibrium world. As new structures form we find the future not playing the same role as the past.

One striking and popular example of the appearance of new structures in the far-from-equilibrium situations is a so-called chemical clock.[9] Ideally we have a chemical reaction whose state we control through appropriate injection of chemical products and elimination of waste products. Suppose that two of the intermediate components of a reaction are respectively formed by red and blue molecules in comparable quantities. We would expect to observe a blurred violet mixture of the two colors with perhaps occasionally some flash of red or blue spots. This is, however, not what happens. In appropriate conditions we see periodically in sequence the whole bottle become red, then blue, then red again. We have a chemical clock.

In a sense, this phenomenon violates all our intuition about chemical reactions being produced by molecules moving in a disordered fashion and colliding at random. In principle each molecule would know only what its direct neighbors are doing. Yet in contrast, the existence of a chemical clock shows that, far from being chaotic, the behavior of the intermediate components of red and blue are highly coherent. In a sense the molecules have to be able to "communicate" in order to synchronize their periodic change of color. In other words, we deal here with new super-molecular scales, both in time and in space, produced by chemical activity. Time scales for these structures are of the order of minutes and space structures may be of the order of centimeters or millimeters, more like the order of biological than of molecular structures.

The mathematical theory for these phenomena is now a rapidly growing field called bifurcation theory. In Figure 2 we see the appearance of such a bifurcation point which may lead to radically new behavior in space and time. We have here a mathematical solution X of chemical equations as a function of some parameter, say λ, which measures, let us say, distance from equilibrium. We see the classic "thermodynamic" solution which is stable up to some critical point λ_c along the plot of a control parameter λ. This situation of stability occurs in equilibrium and near-equilibrium worlds. When the solution becomes unstable and new solutions emerge along branches b_1 and b_2 we have far-from-equilibrium conditions. Note that extrapolation of the "classic thermodynamic" branch, a^1, is unstable beyond λ_c. The critical point at

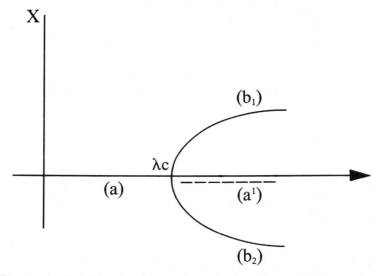

Figure 2. A typical bifurcation diagram representing instability and appearance of new solutions. The branch (a) becomes unstable at the point λc at which two new stable solutions (b_1) and (b_2) bifurcate. The continuation of the branch (a), denoted by (a'), is unstable.

which this occurs, λ_c, is called the point of bifurcation and new time scales occur, like the chemical clock, or new length scales. For example, the two branches b_1 and b_2 of Figure 2 may correspond to the non-uniform distribution of concentration X in a one-dimensional medium so that we see in Figure 3(a) the concentration of X is larger at the left and in Figure 3(b) it is larger at the right. We see that we can have either a left or right "structure." The choice between the two possibilities involves a basically random element. No additional information, whatever the precision, can predict which of the two branches will be selected, at least when we move along the classic thermodynamic branch increasing progressively the value of λ. The selection of one of the branches corresponds to a unique event which is later amplified by autocalytic behavior (such kind of mechanism has often been invoked to understand the dominance of a particular form of optical activity in present day bio-polymers). However, if we repeat the experiment, we are likely to restore symmetry by selection of the other branch. We shall return to the question of pattern selection below.

The first bifurcation introduces a single time or space parameter which can break the time or space symmetry of a system. But this is

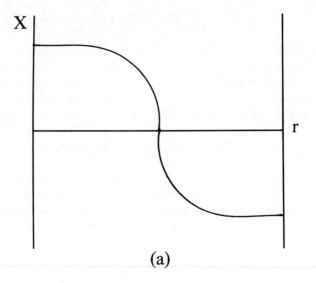

(a)

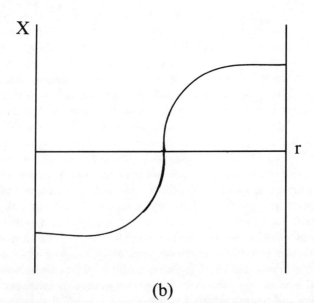

(b)

Figure 3. Dissipative structures corresponding to the bifurcation diagram shown in Fig. 2 in a one-dimensional system. The variations of the concentration of X with position r are shown, one corresponding to the branch (b_1), the other to (b_2).

only the start. There are many bifurcations, generally giving rise to successively more complex patterns, to new scales of time or of length. And what is interesting is that the type of behavior of the systems becomes very sensitive to outside conditions. For example in Figure 4 we see a sequence of time behaviors which have been observed in a chemical reaction, the so-called Belousov–Zhabotinskii reaction, in which you see appearing a uniform time-independent solution and then the periodic chemical clock.[10,11] As the distance from equilibrium increases more complicated associations occur and you have chaos appearing, that is, irregular and highly fluctuating motion. This can be followed by a new type of periodic motion or relaxation. What is interesting is that when one continues this investigation one finds regions of order followed by regions of chaos; regions of chaos again followed by regions of order and so on. So the sensitivity of this far-from-equilibrium system is much greater than the sensitivity of equilibrium systems. We can say that matter in far-from-equilibrium conditions acquires basically new properties: the possibility of communication over macroscopic times and distances, the possibility of "perceiving" small effects leading to a pattern selection and, finally, the possibility of memory corresponding again to temporal successions of bifurcations. It is interesting that these types of properties have in the past been always attributed to "living" systems. We see that to some extent they may even apply to "non-living" systems.

The preceding example was about periodic variations in time. Now in Figure 5 we see an example of periodic variations in space. These so-called trigger waves are propagating waves in chemical media under far-from-equilibrium conditions and would never exist in near-equilibrium systems. These propagating waves are similar to the type of communication of signals which is found in many biological systems; for example, like in the aggregation of slime molds. This is one of the reasons why this phenomenon of aggregation in slime molds is under intense investigation today.

Figure 6 is an amusing example of a bifurcation in the world of social insects. Some of my co-workers together with a group of biologists in Brussels are involved in experiments in which they put a nest of ants or termites in one side of a box, along with two symmetrical holes in a partition for roads to some food on the other side of the partition.[12] The purpose of the experiment is to study the path of the ants to the food. In Figure 7 we see the probability, P, plotted which is a function of the number of ants to enter one particular hole. We find initially, as you

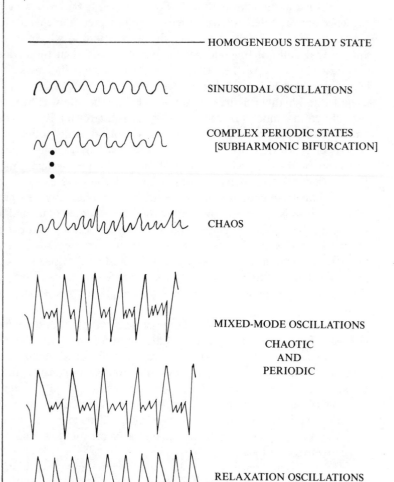

Figure 4. Sequence of different types of oscillatory behavior in the Belousov–Zhabotinskii system as it is driven away from equilibrium.

Figure 5. Trigger waves in Belousov–Zhabotinskii reaction.

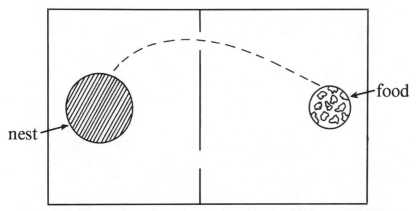

Figure 6. Bifurcation in social systems. The ants have two possible paths to transport food. Beyond a certain critical population the ants choose one of the two possible paths from the food to the nest.

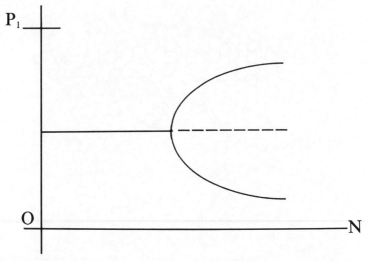

Figure 7. Bifurcation diagram corresponding to behavior of the ants shown in Fig. 6.

would expect, the probability to find one path or the other is the same. However, each ant by choosing a path leaves a signal inviting the other ants to follow the same path. When the number of ants traveling becomes sufficiently large, some critical population of the nest, the signal drives all the ants into using the same path, and the other path is a very small probability. Figures 6 and 7 are a bit schematic, but they present the essentials of the real world experiment.[12] This is another example of how bifurcation appears in the biological world.

The Bénard instability is another striking example of the instability of a stationary state giving rise to a phenomenon of spontaneous organization. In Figure 8 you see a photograph taken from above of a shallow dish of liquid which is heated from below. At first, as heat is propagated from below by conduction, there is no structure of this type but a uniform liquid. However, at some value of the vertical temperature gradient a characteristic structure appears, a kind of non-equilibrium crystal in which millions and millions of molecules move coherently forming hexagonal convection cells of a characteristic size. What is so interesting here is that you have the manifestation of two fundamental elements in nature, non-equilibrium, because the system is in a temperature gradient, and gravitation. As the bottom of the dish is heated the density of the liquid becomes higher near the top than the bottom causing the instability and gravitation comes into play. Normally gravitation in a

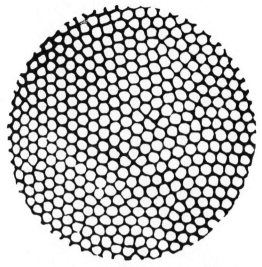

Figure 8. Bénard convection pattern. When a liquid is heated from below, beyond a certain critical temperature, patterns such as this spontaneously form.

small dish a few millimeters thick has little effect as it is washed away by random fluctations. Here on the contrary, the effect of gravitation is magnified because of the far-from-equilibrium conditions. And the same effect can be shown for electrical and magnetic fields. In other words non-equilibrium systems permit matter to "feel" much more in detail the various fields in which it is embedded, be they gravitational, electrical or magnetic. That certainly has to be one of the roads which matter had to follow in order to come to the highly adaptive systems which are the living systems we know.[13,14]

Today many people are involved in the study of not just one bifurcation but of successive changes, that is, sequences of bifurcation. One interesting example which has been studied extensively is the so-called Feigenbaum sequence,[15] an example of which is shown in Figure 9. First there is one single solution which bifurcates into four, sixteen, more and more, until there are an infinite number of branches. This infinite number of frequencies gives an impression of chaos.

So, in a sense, we go along a road from thermal disorder to order, as I explained before in the example of the chemical clock; but we go further in this sequence along the road by also going from order to chaos. However, the word *chaos* is taken here in two different meanings. We start with "thermal" chaos with only molecular wavelengths and

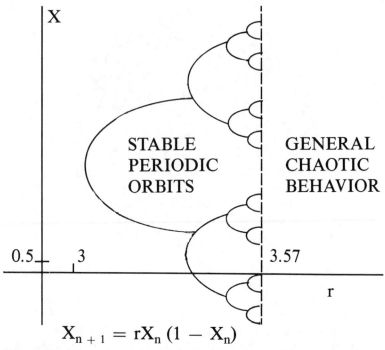

Figure 9. One of the roads to a chaotic behavior—through successive bifurcation. X represents a population, r is a parameter. The population in the $(n + 1)^{\text{th}}$ generation $X_{n + 1}$ is determined by the population X_n of the nth generation according to the equation $X_{n+1} = rX_n(1 - X_n)$.

times, and we come to "macroscopic chaos" in which many macroscopic times or lengths coexist. More generally the word *chaos* sounds to me quite ambiguous. For example, someone recently asked me whether a tropical forest represents chaos or order? I did not know. In a tropical forest you might have appearing an enormous number of time scales and characteristic lengths. And it may well be that what one sees as chaos in fact corresponds to a very complicated system that is highly organized. Therefore such questions are not easy to answer. What I wish to emphasize here is that the Feigenbaum sequence is a possible road to what people today often call chaos.

An example of the occurrence of bifurcation in hydrodynamics is the so-called Taylor instability. In this experiment a rotating wave pattern appears in a liquid when an inner cylinder rotates with respect to an outer one. As the velocity is increased there is first the appearance of rotation, Figure 10(a), and then through successive bifurcations the liquid begins to oscillate more and more, both transversely and longitudinally as in Figures 10(b) and 10(c). Finally a more complicated appearance occurs as in Figure 10(d). This phenomenon corresponds to a road to higher and higher disorder as manifested by the existence of more and more frequencies. While the pattern formation involves irreversible processes, the transition from laminar to turbulent flow remains "invertible." When we change the bifurcation parameter (which is essentially the flow rate), we go from one structure to the other and vice versa. But that is not always so.

Take for example in biology the spatial organization of different cell types, which is the problem of patterns of formation or morphogen-

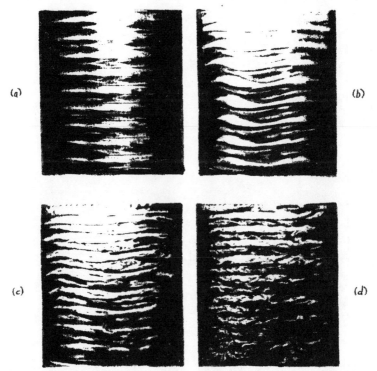

(a)

(b)

(c)

(d)

Figure 10. Taylor instability. When a fluid is placed in between two concentric cylinders, one of which is rotating, beyond a certain critical speed of revolution vortex patterns such as these can be observed. The succession of patterns corresponds to increasing speed of revolution.

esis. It is interesting to think about how cells may be differentiated which at first all appear to have the same role. People have developed models of successive bifurcations like that shown in Figure 11 which increase diversity and give order and specialization to the sequences of cells which form in a given time.[14] Such models lead to the calculation of wavelengths which become unstable in succession when the size of the system increases (see Fig. 11). Of course, the size of a system is here very important. It is here the bifurcation parameter. It is when the system is growing, for example in an embryo, that cells are developing and we expect more and more differentiation. This idea of cell differentiation as a consequence of bifurcation is today quite popular.[16,17] In Figure

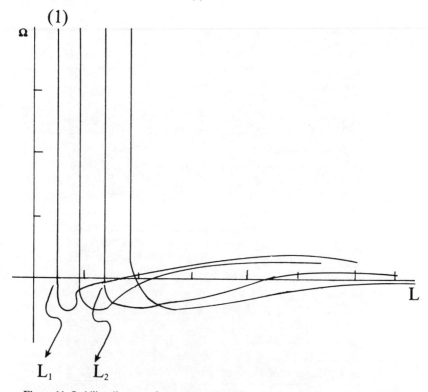

Figure 11. Stability diagram of structures with different wave numbers. The bifurcation parameter here is the size L. For L smaller than L_1 and larger than L_2 the structure (1) is unstable. Similarly for the other structures.

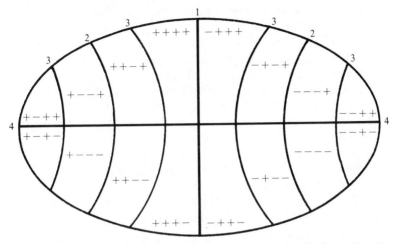

Figure 12. Development of Drosophila Melanogaster. Compartmentalization predicted by diffusion-reaction model. Each compartment is specified by a binary code. Transdetermination predicted on the basis of the change in the binary code.

12 we see the type of results obtained by Kauffman and coworkers at the University of Pennsylvania. They have shown that much of the data in differentiation of drosophila may be understood in terms of bifurcations which occur in the embryo giving different regions or territories in it.[17] The plus sign means that a bifurcation, let us say, increased the content of some chemical in a region and the minus sign means that there was a decrease. As bifurcations occur more and more regions become differentiated, and remarkable predictions have been made. For example, if matter is transferred from one region plus, plus, plus to another region of plus, plus, plus one obtains a normal development. But if matter is transferred from a plus, minus, minus region to a plus, plus, plus, plus region then one expects a monster. You expect that the regions are not equivalent and therefore something unusual will happen to the developing organism. Kauffman made many successful predictions of this type for drosophila. This is a remarkable achievement and shows another road of sequences which is opposite in a sense to the road of Feigenbaum, as shown in Figure 9. The road here leads to more and more order; indeed, it leads to the morphological organization of a living system. Moreover here we can no longer go in an arbitrary direction. As

mentioned, the bifurcation parameter is the size which *increases* irreversibility with time.

Of course, I do not think we have covered the full story. Other elements must also play an important role in evolution, especially in pre-biological evolution. All the systems I have considered here are systems in which essentially the reactions or the hydrodynamic equations were given once for all. I think what really characterizes biological or social evolution is that new elements appear, new molecules appear, new inventions appear, and with them new types of behavior. And this leads to a type of instability which I have only time to mention. It is often called structural instability, in which one must watch the reaction of a system for the appearance of new "functions," or, in the world of chemistry, for new molecules. That phenomenon is probably going to play a more important role for the fascinating questions of evolution of life in its pre-biological stages and social diversification. Evolution in a non-trivial sense requires a continued interaction between the "microscopic" and the "macroscopic" level. This aspect is obvious on the ecological and sociological levels where individuals and macroscopic features (such as institutions . . .) are engaged in a complex dialectical process. However, we are still far from a precise formulation of this idea on the biological level. Whatever this may be, thermodynamic macroscopic concepts, as well as the idea of evolution, of an anisotropy of time, appear on all levels: from the level of elementary particles up to the level of cosmology. This is not due to some arbitrary choice to follow a new intellectual fashion; rather it is imposed on us by new experimental knowledge.

III

In the second section of this talk, I described a chemical clock and other experiments which have changed our concepts about the organization of matter in non-equilibrium conditions. On the cosmological scale there is also a crucial experiment which has drastically changed our view about the evolution of matter. This is the discovery of residual black body radiation, that the world is full of photons at the temperature of three degrees Kelvin. In terms of the history of the universe this can only be understood to correspond to a kind of fossil radiation which has survived from an early period when matter and radiation were in equilibrium. This equilibrium was disrupted by the cosmological expansion and corresponding cooling of the universe. What is so extraordinary about this discovery is that thermodynamics and time now enter into the basic description of matter. The traditional view was that time is essential for understanding living systems, including societies, but the existence of fossils in the context of the non-living physical world was something quite unexpected. This discussion can be extended. For example, take the idea that there are particles and anti-particles. Why, after all, is there an excess of particles over anti-particles? Why is there any matter at all? This is often considered to be the result of a non-equilibrium situation which arose at the earliest stage after the formation of photons. Thus even in these fields of cosmology we come to a new type of concept in which equilibrium and non-equilibrium play a role. Within this perspective the most recent predictions are that all matter is unstable. And probably at some point in the future we shall understand also how matter can originate from photons, from light. Therefore the Lucretian view of permanent elements is now more and more being replaced by a chemical view in which matter is transformed into light and light into matter. All this goes on by means of the two competing driving forces of gravitation and entropy.

IV

I have tried to show that the emphasis on time has brought in unifying elements which connect science and culture more closely together, as Teilhard predicted. And in science itself, it is already certain that none of the three basic levels (the level of elementary particles, the molecular and biochemical level, and the cosmological level) can be considered in isolation. Each of them depends on the two others. Most of the questions which we ask are still left unsolved. However, perspectives now are quite different from the past.

As I said, in Teilhard there is a prophetic element which goes beyond science proper. But it is remarkable that his position appears today much less isolated than it was at the time of his writing. In a beautiful article on the energy of the universe Freeman Dyson has written, "It is conceivable however that life may have a larger role to play than we have yet imagined. Life may succeed against all of the odds in molding the universe to its own purpose. And the design of the inanimate universe may not be as detached from the potentialities of life and intelligence as scientists of the twentieth century have tended to suppose."[18]

Let me close with a personal remark. In December of 1980 a number of scientists were invited to meet in Rome, first with Cardinal Koenig and then with Pope John Paul. We scientists were asked to prepare a short paper to be presented to John Paul. John Paul responded with a discourse dealing with the relations between science and religion which I shall not analyze here. But let me simply mention the beginning of the paper which we prepared. It notes: "Scientists are engaged in a highly creative and ethical activity in their efforts to understand the natural world, including ourselves. The coming together of science, culture and spiritual activity is necessary for the fulfillment of human needs. The world is presently in a difficult period of adjustment, and we urge people to be patient in judging what the longer term future will be like. The complexity of this adjustment renders the future's possibilities very uncertain. But the role of science in this situation is essential for human survival." What I want to emphasize is that this characterization of science as a creative and ethical activity which is embedded in culture as a whole, puts science in the frame of other human activities, and again emphasizes the convergence of interest which is characteristic of the work of Teilhard. It is in strong contrast with the views in which science finally has to come in conflict with society and culture. You may have heard about the remarkable play by Duerrenmatt, "The Physicists." In this play three physicists, the central characters of the play, discuss the basic ways and means of advancing physics and at the same time safeguarding mankind from the dire consequences of the political powers appropriating the results of its progress. The conclusion they reach is that the only possible way is that already chosen by one of them. They all decide to go on pretending to be mad, to hide in the midst of a lunatic asylum. At the end of the play, as fate would have it, their last refuge is discovered to be an illusion. The woman director of the asylum spies on her patient, steals his results and seizes the world power.

The problems raised by this play, the danger for the survival of humanity which may arise from scientific progress cannot be minimized. Still we have no choice. Whatever the responsibility of the past, science, politics based on imperialism, and other factors, the situation as it stands today requires a close collaboration between science and the humanities to insure the dignity of human life for the expanding population of tomorrow. It is in this global perspective that I believe that the pioneering work of Teilhard de Chardin appears in full light. And the lesson which I would like to retain from the study of complex systems is that such systems are never stable. Such systems can always go into new configuration, always become destabilized and restructured by new fluctuations. In other words, for sufficiently complex systems, perhaps humanity and perhaps the world itself, there will be no end to history.

NOTES

1. I. Berlin, *Against the Current,* selected writings edited by H. Hardy (New York: The Viking Press, 1980), p. XXVI.
2. L. Lévy-Bruhl, *La Mentalité Primitive* (P.U.F., 1922).
3. J. Monod, *Chance and Necessity* (New York: Vintage Books, 1972), pp. 172–173.
4. I. Prigogine, "Einstein: Triumphs and Conflicts," Albert Einstein: Four Commemorative Lectures (Austin: The Humanities Research Center, 1979).
5. P. A. Schilpp, editor, *The Philosophy of Rudolf Carnap* (London: Cambridge University Press, 1963).
6. P. Teilhard de Chardin, *Le Phénomène Humain* (Paris: Editions du Seuil, 1955).
7. Lucretius, *De Natura Rerum,* livre I, vers 267–270.
8. The second law summarizes the characteristic features of reversible and irreversible processes. As formulated by Rudolf Clausius in the nineteenth century it considers isolated systems which exchange neither energy nor matter with the outside world. The law implies the existence of a function S, the entropy, which increases monotonically until it reaches its maximum value at the state of thermodynamic equilibrium:

$$\frac{dS}{dt} \geq 0 \text{ where } t = \text{time}$$

This formulation is easily extended to systems that exchange energy and matter with the outside world, as with the system in Figure 1. The total entropy dS, can be defined as:

$$dS = d_e S + d_i S$$

According to the second law, entropy production inside the system is positive, i.e., $d_i S \geq 0$. It is in this formulation that the basic distinction between reversible and irreversible processes becomes essential. Only irreversible processes contribute to entropy production.

9. Consider two components in a chemical system whose concentrations are plotted in the drawing below. No matter what the initial conditions, the sys-

tem takes a periodic orbit. In other words X and Y vary periodically in time. This is only possible in an open system which is driven by an appropriate flow of matter. Chemical clocks have been described in many books and popular articles. [See I. Prigogine, *From Being to Becoming* (San Francisco: W. H. Freeman and Co., 1980)]

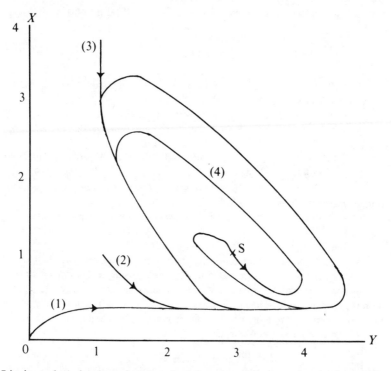

Limit cycle behavior of a chemical reaction. The same periodic trajectory is obtained for different initial conditions. The letter S represents unstable steady state. [See ref. 10]

10. G. Nicolis and I. Prigogine, *Self-Organization in Nonequilibrium Systems—From Dissipative Structures to Order through Fluctuations* (New York: John Wiley Interscience, 1977).

11. J. S. Turner, et al., Physics Lett. (1981) in press; also, J. C. Roux, et al., in *Nonlinear Problems: Present and Future,* Proc. of Conf. at Los Alamos (1981) A. R. Bishop, ed. (Amsterdam: North-Holland, 1981).

12. J. L. Deneubourg, private communication.

13. D. K. Kondepudi and I. Prigogine, "Sensitivity of Nonequilibrium Systems," Physica *107A* (1981) 1–24.

14. G. Nicolis and I. Prigogine, PNAS (USA) *78* (1981) 659–663.

15. See, for example, "Period-Doubling Route to Chaos Shows Universality," Physics Today (March, 1981) 17–19.

16. Raima Larter and Peter Ortoleva, J. Theor. Biol. *88* (1981) 599.

17. Stuart A. Kauffman, Ronald M. Shymko, Kenneth Trabert, "Control of Sequential Compartment Formation in *Drosophila,*" Science *199* (1978) 259–270.

18. Freeman J. Dyson, "Energy in the Universe," Scientific American *225* (1971) 50–59.

SUMMARY OF RESPONSE AND DISCUSSION

Dr. John O'Keefe responded by giving some examples from his own work in physics and astronomy that exemplify the irreversible processes described by Prigogine. Scientists have long puzzled over scratches on tektites, glassy pebbles that are found in space. O'Keefe told how Prigogine's derivations of irreversible asymmetrical situations from symmetry in nature can explain these scratches. This showed a unity of knowledge within science.

O'Keefe then applied Prigogine's discussion of entropy and the second law of thermodynamics in the universe to man's contemporary experience of global communication. He proposed that information is negative entropy.

Looking towards the future, we at least hope that the communication net which is extending all over the world will help to bring about the Omega Point to bring people closer together.

Soleri asked about the place of God in this new chemical vision of the universe; and an intervention from the floor questioned whether there seems to be a built-in teleology in the process of complexification. Prigogine responded:

Why is there an evolution at all? At the moment we can only propose an answer on a limited time scale. And there is no doubt that the motor behind evolution is the cosmological evolution with all the bifurcations and selections between chance and randomness. Here I think that Teilhard clearly went beyond what science can say. There is a kind of hope or surmise that in some way the direction of evolution is fixed and is a road to some perfection. That is different from the conclusions that I could take from my studies in which there is indeed no end to history, but also no global view of history that can be formulated *a priori*.

4

Human Unity: Past and Future

Richard E. Leakey

I must confess that to stand here before you—having listened with you to so much that I did not understand—fills me with fear. However I believe that I can address myself to the central purpose of this meeting: namely, to build upon and take forward some of the ideas and concepts that are so well encompassed in the writings of Teilhard. I have to confess that for various reasons I have not read a great deal of Teilhard. But I do know that Teilhard was concerned with an issue that clearly concerns all of the speakers and probably all of the listeners at this extraordinary meeting. I think the meeting is particularly important today in a world that knows a constant crisis—crises that can be brought right into your homes through the extraordinary systems of communication. It is a world wherein we are facing extraordinary dangers in terms of the survival of our species. It is fitting that we should bring the thinking, the aim towards survival, closer together. But in this conservative world, this world that is perhaps more polarized now than it has been for some years (particularly in the West), we see a retreat back to ultra-conservatism. We see people speaking about the contradictions between science and religion; we see people questioning the value of science for the solution of human problems; and there are some who say that if you are a scientist you cannot really be involved with the humanities, and vice versa. For me, nothing could be further from the truth. Both science and religion are dynamic pursuits, and in their very dynamism there must be a bringing together.

I speak of religion and science in the broadest possible sense. I realize that most of you who have gathered for this weekend are Christians. But there is *other* religion, great religion, which is concerned with the same thing as Christianity: namely, a system of beliefs, a system of bonding people together so that they have confidence, not only in themselves, but in their neighbors, so that they can operate as a social system.

We read philosophy, but we seldom hear philosophy. And this reminds me of one of the great problems that we as human beings face today. So much wisdom, so many extraordinary insights into the planet, into ourselves and our relationship to all about us, is held by people who cannot write. Yesterday we mentioned the great Eastern and Western philosophies. But nothing was said of the great philosophies of the indigenous people of the New World, this continent and South America. Seldom do we think of the great philosophies that now exist in their original form in the great continent of Africa or among the aboriginal people of Australia. There are many people who belong to the same species as ourselves, who think of life and its meaning, but who have not had the opportunity to express it in documents that can be spread around the world. Now through the revolution in communication this issue can be addressed. And much of the wisdom that exists in this world can be shared and all can benefit.

We are all concerned with a quest for the truth. I was taught by my father—who was certainly the most important person in my life—that absolute truth is the most elusive part of human experience. In my presence as a child he frequently explained to visitors his concept of the difference between relative and absolute truth as it pertained to his own work: namely, the study of the past through an investigation of the fossil evidence. His approach was very simple: he would take from his pocket a matchbox. Now I do not have a matchbox because I have at least one virtue. But if I were to hold up this box while hiding from you all sides but one, you could each describe it accurately in the same way. But if I were to turn it around to a different perspective, you would give a very different description, but one that is also accurate. And if I were to open this box you would get another view. Each of your descriptions would be true. Now I believe that the work of mathematicians, engineers, architects, philosophers, theologians and all of us is concerned with a simple question: What it's all about? I say, "What it's all about?"

because I am concerned with the arrogance that often prevails in human discussion; we universalize our own concerns. We are but a part of what it is all about. The totality of life and its systems on the planet, and even the relation of this planet to other systems is perhaps itself not the complete box but still only a view.

I am also concerned that we can sit in the audience today understanding what is said accepting some statements and rejecting others. But when did we start thinking and at what level do we have this capacity for thought? I believe that by studying human origins from the paleontological perspective we can in fact move closer to an awareness that our uniqueness today is real; but its origin or genesis has been very gradual and is related to time and instabilities. I find it intriguing to take us, homo sapiens, and to look at us in terms of how we came to be what we are. Because by understanding where we have come from and what we are I believe we have a better basis for dealing with the future.

Many people have expressed concern that evolution has not been proven. Now I do not want to take a lot of your time discoursing on that subject, but I would like to take advantage of the means of mass communication available to me today to say that there is no doubt at all that evolution is a fact. We are here today because of evolution. There is, of course, room to discuss the mechanism by which it happened, and that is my professional interest. I want to know when it was, why it was and how it was that an organism was transformed over a period of time. That organism is ourselves: an organism that can stand up, that can talk, that can think. What was the pressure that led to the selection of greater intelligence? What was the pressure that led to the use of technology? What was the pressure that led to the development of bi-pedalism? What was the cause of extinction of several other humanoid species in the past? What is the meaning of our present situation in terms of this coming together of the conscious world, the philosophical world? These are the sort of questions that can be answered.

If we look at ourselves and at others, there is no doubt that we find a diversity. There is a diversity of physical appearance, diversity of culture and a diversity of thought. Let us first concern ourselves with physical differences. If you have more pigment than someone else and less than another; if you have a wider, flatter nose while others have a nose that is pointed and narrow, if you are tall or short, if you run well or do not run well—these can all be related to environmental situations. Cultural differences can also be explained on the basis of environmental isolation wherein attitudes have developed without much mixing. And indeed, as a result of improved communication we are seeing a dissipation of that today. Religious attitudes also are a result of this mind of ours that enables us to be religious.

It is easy to speak of the present, but when we speak of the past the element of time makes our judgments more difficult. One of the issues that is brought up is that paleontologists cannot agree with themselves. You read of their arguments in the newspapers. Of course this is true, because none of the pieces of evidence we draw from the past, the natural fossils as opposed to the physical fossils, come with labels. If they did, I assure you we would tell you how to read them. We attach labels to them because we wish to organize them and talk about them in a meaningful way. You can find skulls or skeletons of humans that lived forty or sixty thousand years ago, and these are clearly human. They are the sort of skulls that we have today or that anyone in the world would have today. And we can follow our species back, in terms of the bony parts, to a distance of a hundred thousand years. We can trace our genus, homo, back a couple of million years; that is, we can trace our human family back four million years. Now whether we ourselves are human is purely up to us to decide. And whether something else is human is also purely up to us to decide. I think one of the challenges that a man with the breadth of vision of Teilhard might deal with is the problem of labeling things through the course of time. There is a system of labeling called taxonomy systematics wherein one describes sub-species or races, species, genera and so forth. This great system was worked out by Linnaeus over two hundred years ago. It did not account for change through time. And one of the great difficulties that scientists face today in understanding the natural order is relating the supposed immutability of species with the concept of evolution. So when we take the fossil record and attempt to make order out of it—there must be order because we are human—we impose on it a system that must be faulty because it does not allow for the passage of time. I am not in a position to offer a solution; I merely raise this issue to explain why paleontology is so complicated today and this is particularly true of paleoanthropology. We as thinking beings are imposing our concepts on nature, and we have not redefined the system we are using to take into account the new knowledge that is part of the dynamism of science.

When we become concerned with our presence on the planet, we become concerned with why we behave the way we do. And human behavior is an area that concerns me very much. It is possible to document human behavior back through time for over two million years. If last night our reception room had been left exactly as it was, people coming into the room would have been able to determine fairly accurately what had happened there yesterday evening. From the cups, plates, cookies, crackers and cheese on the floor people could not be able to determine what we were discussing, but they would have been able to determine that we were in a crowd in which we were not paying much attention to eating, because there was a good deal of it lying around. You can go to Williamsburg, in nearby Virginia, and find the remains of houses, of stockades, of places where your forebears lived. And you are able to do this by interpreting what is left behind—basically, litter. And the most interesting part of an archeological career is the pursuit of garbage. Without garbage, without the propensity of our species to discard things, there would be no place for archeologists. The further back you go the more limited you are, for many objects do not stand the passage of time. Metal objects will rust in five-hundred or a thousand years. Leather objects, unless it is very dry, will disappear. Wooden objects will often have rotted, unless conditions for preservation were perfect. Many things that are a part of ordinary life and from which we can interpret life-styles vanish. In finds from the recent past you can sometimes supplement what you find by the written word. The further back you go the less likelihood of finding anything preserved unless it was made of stone. Nevertheless, it is possible to learn a great deal from the archeological record, and much of what I will say in the remaining part of my address will concern what has been gleaned from the pre-historic record.

Some prehistorians have allowed us to believe that there is a strong element of violence in our species. We can certainly look around the world today and see violence in tragic examples, terrifying examples of the way people behave towards other humans. Our comic books are filled with pictorial representations of violence. Often the comics attribute violence to ancestral types, ape-men, hairy creatures. We have all seen drawings of the cave man with the club dragging a woman by the neck back to a cave—for whatever purpose. Yesterday I was talking to a child of a very well educated family. And I said to the child, age eleven, "What is your favorite activity?" "Oh," he said, "shooting down people." I said, "Shooting down people? What sort of people are you shooting?" "Oh," he said, "all sorts. I blow them off; I blow them off the world." I suddenly realized that he was not talking about people, but images of people, people whom he could blow up on these extraordinary television screens whereon by pushing a series of buttons you can activate bombs and grenades and flame-throwers and all such dreadful things. That child has grown up with the belief that violence is a natural part of life. It is fun; it is fun to kill. But where does that come from? That was not handed down by the Lord; it is not a divine part of our existence. Where has it come from? It has come from us. We have created this environment. But many people have justified it on the basis that our ancestors had this similar propensity. Fortunately our ancestors did not have TV games. But it has been argued that if you look at the fossils you find skulls that have been smashed open. It has been argued that one can find collections of bones that have been broken in such a way that would clearly indicate they were being used as weapons. Thus, violence is attributed to man over millions of years. Now I have argued fervently about this. If you look at the archeological record there is no justification for such a position. The breakages that you see in every single fossil bone up until about thirty-thousand years ago can best be explained as a natural breakage or breakage by carnivores and scavengers. I know of not a single fossil from Africa in the early periods of our past that shows evidence of violence. I do not know of a single weapon in the archeological record of the far distant past. And when weapons do come in, they were weapons that were used for obtaining protein. Now when you pull up a potato to get its root or kill an ox to get its meat, you are feeding yourself. And this is a very different thing than the aggression that we find in Northern Ireland, in Cambodia, in Uganda, and in many parts of the world. The present propensity to organize ourselves to destroy ourselves in large numbers has nothing to do with the hunting for food that surely has been a part of our heritage.

If you accept that there is no evidence for aggression and violence in the past, what evidence is there that man the hunter, the "killer ape," was the driving force of human evolution? I say man the hunter, because it is the male who hunts. If the hunting theory of evolution were true, many of you would have to live in the dismal situation of knowing that the success of your species had nothing to do with your sex. I am speaking, of course, of the women. The image of man the hunter, though it may be powerful and prevalent with the macho males that strut around the world today, has no relevance to present society. If we look at the archeological record in Africa from one million to two million years ago, it is quite clear that meat (at least initially) was brought back to the campsites to be eaten. But from the evidence that we find—in terms of the species represented and the ages of the animals—our meat-eating ancestors were scavenging. They were going out to steal meat from the more successful hunters—not other people, but lions, tigers and hyenas. Stealth and cunning (theft if you like, although I prefer to think of it as scavenging) were an important part of strategy. From scavenging you can become dependent upon meat-eating as a part of life. Then, if the predators are not predating well enough to satisfy your needs, it is not a difficult step to begin hunting on your own. This is particularly true if you have developed an intelligent brain.

Consider now that you are eating meat. You are eating something that you can share. Berries, nuts and fruit come in little packages. Imagine the peanuts that you might have had at last night's reception. They are little objects. If you were collecting peanuts in the wild, the last thing you would want to do would be to share one with your colleague. It is such a little morsel. But if in walking across the plains I come upon a wild beast or a buffalo upon whom the lions have gorged themselves and left the remains for lesser scavengers, it is not difficult for me to take some meat myself. And, providing I have some means of detaching it, I can take back a package of meat that is much larger than I can eat myself. I can now share what I have with others. And I believe that this food-sharing, this returning home with food that could be shared, was perhaps the most important strategy in the development of our species. It is this that gave rise to a way of life that is uniquely human in the primate world. Thus, I see meat-eating leading to food-sharing, and food-sharing leading ultimately to a division of labor and all the things that go with it: the learning process, kinship and family groupings.

Now I would like to bring you back again to an issue that concerns me. I believe we are what we are because of what has been. I find it difficult to visualize ourselves as the inevitable consequence of evolution. We are the consequence of a series of events, and it is possible to study those events and to document some of them. That is a first point. I think that if we accept that we are not an inevitability, that we are merely at the end of a particular branch on a bush rather than at the pinnacle of a tree, we can begin to understand better some of the issues that today threaten the survival of mankind. I am deeply concerned that today more than ever before there is the possibility for the extinction of our species. This extinction can occur in a number of ways. It can be brought about by uncontrolled nuclear conflict. This is not something hypothetical; the weaponry already exists. I do not see this as likely at the present time as the nuclear arms are in the hands of societies that have too much to lose by the conflict. Nevertheless, those same societies have much to gain from countries in parts of the world that do not have the same technology. And this brings us to the North-South conflict that I see increasingly coming into focus today. If you want oil, rubber, uranium, copper, or whatever, the chances are that the underdeveloped parts of the world, the Southern world, will to some extent be where it is. And countries desperate to maintain a way of life will often buy with what they have at their disposal. We already see the ugly prospect of nuclear arms in parts of the world where perhaps there is less to lose. I think this is dangerous.

I also think that it is dangerous that we are consciously destroying the environment that supports life. It is clear that we cannot and must not allow ourselves to be beguiled into thinking that one group or another group has a right to survive at the expense of the others. We must not think that as a nation or as a group of nations we are independent. This is not viable. If we are going to control the destruction of the seas, the pollution of the waters, the misuse of antibiotics and drugs, the evolutionary development of disease, then we must approach this control not on the basis of the survival of America, or Kenya, or Britain, or Australia, but on the basis of the survival of our species. To do that we must accept that we are a single species. Though your skin might have more or less pigment, though your hair might be more or less flaxen or curly, you are part of the same species. I believe we can show this. You surely have the same destiny. And I believe what is needed is to bring together people to look upon the future of our species on the basis of our species. We are one. And I am sure that the work of Teilhard was a pioneering work in trying to convey this oneness.

I believe that it is dangerous to assume or to believe that this unity can be achieved on the basis of a single religion. And I take issue with the idea that there is a right and a wrong way to worship. I take issue with those who say that it is wrong to believe in one God, you should believe in six. And I take issue with those who say you should worship six and not one. There is a need for understanding the diversities that have sprung up from our common origin. From our diversity we must look beyond a strengthening of the separate component parts. Nationalism and the great religions are all part and parcel of the human experiment. It is my conviction that we are now in a position to go the next step. We are in a position to talk about the origin of man, not on the basis of Genesis or reincarnation, but on the basis of a biological evolution through time. And I believe that we can portray to the young people now in school the story of our origins with the same confidence we portray thermodynamics, aerodynamics, hydrodynamics, gravity, and the basic principles of science. There are certain facts about life that all can share; it is the interpretation of those facts that gives the diversity. But if we have the same facts, we have a better chance for unity. And without this unity our prospects are frightening. And therefore I say that this meeting, where we have the opportunity to discuss a common view of the box from so many professions and disciplines, is a unique opportunity. And I hope there will be more such meetings, because I do care.

SUMMARY OF RESPONSE AND DISCUSSION

Dr. J. S. Weiner's response told of several recent developments that would have been of great interest to Teilhard: the DNA molecule, the spectacular discoveries in African anthropology, and the growing sense for ecology:

> We have reached a point of awareness on a world basis of what the world's resources and particularly its energy resources amount to. We begin to budget what we are gaining and what we are losing. And I think this is particularly in tune with the collective world consciousness, the collective perception, about which Teilhard spoke.

Panikkar began the discussion by objecting to Leakey's image of reality as a box. "Objectification is only a part of a much more complicated process. I do not think that there are pure facts." Heisenberg has shown us that the observation of a fact modifies the fact: "the observer is part of the fact."

Someone from the floor asked Leakey if the present nuclear threat shows a failure of religion. Leakey responded, "I believe a commitment to the survival of the species, a commitment to the proper utilization of the planet, could be an extension of classical religion. If the goal of religion is to lead people to sacrifice and give on a global scale, then the answer is yes." He added that the solution of the current dilemma "must involve an equalization of what societies have, need and can get."

Soleri spoke of inequities among all of the living: "Eat or be eaten." He asked if one day this could change into compassion and a universal resurrection. "If I am eaten today, I believe that tomorrow I will be resurrected somehow, not to be a means any longer, but to be an end." Leakey picked up on the reference to all of life to make a distinction:

> We have become different from the rest of life because of our self-awareness, our consciousness, and our culture. I do not believe that there is any longer an inevitability about humanity in any of its aspects.

5

The Concept of Evolution in the Interaction Between Science and Religion

Kenneth E. Boulding

Evolution is a word of many meanings. In the broadest possible sense it certainly means the image that we have of the total past and presumably the future of the whole universe. This takes us from the initial "big bang," through the appearance of the elements, radiation, and then compounds, to the aggregation of the stars and galaxies, the formation of the earth, the formation of DNA and the history of living organisms, leading to the human history, up to the present, and continuing beyond into the future.

Evolution, however, is more than a mere description of the universe in space and time; it is also a theory. It is not only a description of what we think happened but at least some account of how it happened, though it does not usually go so far as raising the question of why did it happen. The "how" of evolution begins with the concepts of an ecosystem of interacting populations of different species, which may be physical, chemical, biological, or societal, that is, humans and their artifacts. Populations have additions (births) and subtractions (deaths), whether these are populations of hydrogen atoms, water molecules, biological species, or societal species. When births exceed deaths the population will grow, when deaths exceed births it will decline. The births and deaths of one population are a function of the size of that population itself and the size of all the other populations with which it is in contact. This gives us an ecosystem with ecological interaction of all species in it with the others. Each species has a "niche" if it has an equilibrium population at which births equal deaths.

Evolution then consists of this constant ecological interaction which may be both cooperative, where an increase in one species increases another, or competitive, where an increase in one species diminishes another, all this taking place, however, under conditions of constant change in the parameters of the system. The ecological interaction is *selection*; the change in parameters is *mutation*. In this process some species survive, some species disappear, and some are transformed into new species which survive. The "survival of the fittest" is an almost empty metaphor, for "fitness" means only "fit to survive," which says only that the surviving survive, which we knew anyway. A better metaphor is the "survival of the fitting"—those species that will fit into a niche in an ecosystem. There are a great many such niches and correspondingly a great many strategies of survival. Darwin's "struggle for existence" was another unfortunate metaphor. Struggle is very rare in the biosphere and on the whole is a source of mostly minor disturbances in human history. What matters for survival is birth and death, and these can be very quiet and unnoticed.

Mutation may take the form simply of cooling off and spreading out, as in pre-biological evolution. In the history of life it mainly takes the form of genetic mutation, a change in the instructions which are contained in DNA. Changes in the parameters of the physical environment, such as soil formation and erosion, change in rainfall, in the composition of the atmosphere, and so on, are also important. In human history it takes the form of new ideas, new technologies, new forms of organization, new forms of human knowledge, new skills of human learning, as well as changes in the physical and biological environment through climate change, extinction of living species, soil changes, deforestation, and so on.

The "noosphere," to use Teilhard's excellent term, is a great ecosystem of interacting species of images, ideas, concepts, metaphors, symbols, words, and phrases which are in the first place the cognitive contents of human minds, to which we should add relevant material artifacts, such as books, blueprints, computers, and libraries. Like all ecosystems these tend to cluster into "habitats." In biology habitats frequently have a spatial connotation, like a coral reef, a prairie field, a pond, or a forest. Many species have niches in more than one habitat. As the parameters change, habitats may expand or contract. In an ice age the tundra expands and the forest contracts. As the earth warms up again the process is reversed.

The noosphere likewise has habitats, which have some spatial characteristics. The species of the noosphere that inhabit a church are somewhat different from those that inhabit a chemical laboratory or biology classroom, a home, a gymnasium, or a barracks. As in the biosphere, the habitats of the noosphere are not exclusive; many species inhabit more than one habitat. The human species, indeed, seems now to be able to inhabit all the biological habitats from the deepest ocean to the moon, thanks to its artifacts. Individuals in different phases of their life and in different roles likewise occupy different habitats in the noosphere. Teilhard himself inhabited, though not always at the same time, the noosphere habitat of the altar, the battlefield, and the paleontology laboratory, field station, and classroom.

Both religion and science are large, complex, and sometimes overlapping clusters of noosphere habitats. Religion is particularly complex and diverse, ranging from the shaman and the medicine man to the Shinto temple, the Buddhist monastery, the Islamic mosque, the storefront Church of God, and the Catholic cathedral. Sometimes we see these habitats expand and contract, as when Christianity expanded into Europe and the Mediterranean world in its first few hundred years, contracted as Islam expanded, and expanded again after Columbus into the Americas, and in the nineteenth century into Africa and Asia.

Scientific habitats are perhaps more unified than those of religion. The periodic table of elements is a universal mandala appearing in every chemistry classroom in every country in the world. Nevertheless, there is still great variety. Science tends to be divided into almost noncommunicating disciplines and even subdisciplines, each with a language of its own, virtually incomprehensible to the non-initiated. It is a rare scientist who combines even two different disciplines successfully.

Something resembling science begins to emerge in human history fairly early, with the Chaldean astronomers and the Greek mathematicians, the great Indian discovery of zero, and folk medicine around the world. As a continuing integrated culture, however, it really begins in Europe with Copernicus, Tycho Brahe, Kepler, Galileo, Newton, and others. It begins with astronomy and classical physics, mechanics, and optics. I am prepared to claim economics as the third or fourth oldest of the sciences, for its basic theoretical structure was set by Adam Smith in THE WEALTH OF NATIONS in 1776. I also argue that Adam Smith's theory of relative price equilibrium is the beginning of ecology, economics being just an ecology of commodities, and his theory of economic development, resting fundamentally on the genetic factor of know-how, expanded through the division of labor, transcended Newton into something that is the beginning of evolutionary thought.

The observational sciences of anatomy, which perhaps can be carried back to Vesalius and Harvey, are somewhat earlier than Adam Smith, and botanical and zoological taxonomy, which begins with Linnaeus, a contemporary of Adam Smith, also have some claims to be "early." Chemistry, however, does not really reach scientific status until Dalton in 1808, geology with Lyell in the 1830s; evolutionary biology comes with Darwin in 1869, and experimental psychology and sociology in the 1870s. One could almost argue that biology only became a science in the last generation with molecular biology and geology achieved the same status with plate tectonics. The idea that somehow the physical sciences came first, then the biological, then the social sciences, is quite unfounded. One evening reading about the economist Malthus gave Darwin the idea of natural selection. Chemistry only became evolutionary in the last generation, and we still know very little about the history of the evolution of chemical compounds.

Evolution is not a single process, for evolution itself evolves. With the advent of DNA and life, evolution passed from its physical–chemical phase into its biological phase. With the advent of the human race, it passed into still another phase, that of societal evolution, which has many similarities to but also profound differences from the earlier phases. In pre-biological evolution of the elements, the compounds, and the stars there is not very much that looks like a "gene," except perhaps a catalyst. With biological evolution the phenomenon of "production"—that is, the capacity of genetic structure and instructions to create an organism—becomes of paramount importance. Even in biological evolution, however, we observe the rise of what can be called "noogenetic" development, which is the transmission of learned structures from one generation to the next.

Societal evolution is dominated by noogenetic development. "Biogenetic" evolution—that is, changes in the genetic instructions contained in DNA—has been relatively unimportant, as there has been very little change in the overall human gene pool, as far as we know, in the last 50,000 years. "Noogenetic" evolution, the development of learned structures in human nervous systems, dominates the whole system, though this is not to deny the effects of gene structure on individual learning potentials. Because of this, the human race has been extraordinarily productive in the formation of artifacts. These originate in the knowledge or know-how structures in the human mind, which in turn are capable of enormous expansion and development.

There are three major types of human artifacts, which might be labeled "material," "organizational," and "personal." Material artifacts range from the first eoliths and flint knives to bread, wine, clothes, houses, cathedrals, and space probes. Sometimes these are produced with the aid of biological genes, like hybrid corn and Pekinese dogs, though up to now all we have been able to do is rearrange existing genes through selection. Now, however, we are beginning to recombine existing genes through recombinant DNA into new genetic structures, although we are still nowhere near synthesizing these from scratch. The possibility of new humanly created biological species, however, is now very much in the air.

Mechanical artifacts, like automobiles, always originate in some kind of human knowledge or know-how, which is their genetic base, just as the origin of the living organism is the know-how contained in the fertilized egg or divided cell. In both biological and human production, whether of the horse or of the automobile, this know-how in the genetic structure has to be able to capture energy, in order to select and transport and transform materials into the improbable shapes and structures of the product. In all processes of production, the know-how or genetic factor is the basic creative one. There are, however, the limiting factors of energy in various forms, material in various forms, space and time, the absence of which may prevent the realization of the potential which is implied in the genetic or know-how factor. It is no good knowing how to do something unless we have the energy, materials, space, and time which are required. But these limiting factors by themselves will never produce a product unless they are organized by the genetic factor.

Organizational artifacts are very rare before the human race. Beaver colonies and dams, and termite nests are perhaps examples, but these are still pretty primitive and their repertoire is extremely limited. The human race almost immediately starts producing a proliferating and expanding network of families, clans, tribes, nations, corporations, churches, political parties, communes, international governmental organizations, and many more. These are also created by human knowledge and know-how. They all owe their origin to some idea in the minds of the founders, followed by complex systems of communication and persuasion. Physical structures are also significant in the way of buildings, furniture, telephones, offices, churches, and lodges.

The size of material and organizational artifacts, both biological and human, depends on the development of certain structural characteristics which determine the point at which diseconomies of scale limit further growth. This in turn depends on the fact that doubling the linear dimensions of any given structure quadruples the areas and octuples the volumes—a 2-inch cube has four times the area and eight times the volume of a 1-inch cube. Some functions of a structure like communication depend on length; some like respiration or digestion happen at surfaces; some like weight depend on volume. Thus, the cell could not be ten times its usual size without collapsing; the development of the stiff exoskeleton in the insect permitted it to be much larger than the cell; the development of the interior endoskeleton permitted another large increase in the size of the organism in reptiles, birds, fish and mammals, culminating in the blue whale. Similarly with human artifacts, the development of the steel-frame building, which is analogous to the endoskeleton, permitted skyscrapers and a great expansion of the size of human structures. The development of electricity and air conditioning had somewhat the same effect on the size of buildings that the development of the lungs and nervous systems did in animals in terms of permitting an expansion of scale.

Persons are partly biological artifacts coming from the fertilized egg and are partly societal artifacts created by communication from and to other human beings in a great inflow and outflow of information. The teaching–learning processes of a culture tend to produce persons through the education and socialization of children that replace the older persons in the culture who pass out of it through death. Americans tend to produce Americans; Chinese, Chinese; Catholics, Catholics; chemistry professors, chemists; and so on, though there are also mutations and exceptions. In my own case, for instance, the English produced an American! Persons are also produced as a result of the enormous internal activity of the human nervous system. We are not passive recipients of information from outside. We are creators of information within us and selectors of information that comes in from outside. Language is a particularly interesting example of a human artifact which has a certain biological base in the sense that the genetically produced human nervous system has a potential for language of some kind.

There is nothing biogenetic, however, about English or Chinese and the language which a person speaks and understands as a native language is entirely a function of the learning process. Even here internal processes of language generation are by no means absent, as anybody who has experienced identical twins can testify.

Persons are grouped into cultures and subcultures, each with a common language, common interests, and a common value system or ethos. Each culture tends to occupy a habitat in both space and time. These may shift as migration takes place—the Pilgrim Fathers to New England or the Jesuit Fathers to Paraguay. Sometimes the location shifts very rapidly as with nomads or motorcycle gangs; sometimes it remains stable for long periods as in a settled village. Each subculture has an ethos—that is, a set of preferences on the part of individuals which defines the membership in the subculture. An individual who does not conform to the ethos either moves toward conforming or leaves the subculture. Any Jesuit who is converted to Zen Buddhism would have considerable difficulty remaining in the community, and a great difficulty would be exhibited by a Zen Buddhist monk who is converted to Catholicism. Nevertheless, cultures are very rarely isolated and there is a constant input into them, not only of new people but of ideas, images, know-how, material artifacts, and many other ways. These may not conform to the existing structure of the culture, so that all cultures inevitably change. The capacity for a culture to change indeed while still retaining a sense of identity with the past is a very important element in survival.

Changes are often perceived as conflicts, especially when they are wanted by some members of the subculture and not by others. Conflicts have a certain tendency to become organized as those persons who perceive themselves as having interests in common are mobilized into "factions" within a larger cultural organization. Organizations in conflict, unfortunately, have a strong tendency to create and to reinforce each other. A good example of this would be national armed forces, which are in an ecological sense cooperative with each other, and each competitive with their own civilian populations. Thus, a growth in the armed force in the Soviet Union produces growth in the armed force in the United States, that produces a further growth in the armed force of the Soviet Union, and so on in an arms race, which can often be extremely detrimental to both parties and could end in war. Organizations indeed often create conflicts which are inimical to the interests of their own members. This is particularly the case where what might be called "negative identities" are created—that is, identities which depend on what one is not rather than what one is. This almost always creates pathological conflict situations in which everybody becomes worse off. The long tragic history of wars, civil strife, and persecutions are testimony to this principle.

The interaction between the scientific subculture and the religious subcultures is very complex, especially in the last 500 years. The scientific subculture, as we have seen, developed first in Europe and is usually dated to Copernicus. One of the very interesting problems in the history of human thought is why science developed in Europe and not, for instance, in China or in the Islamic community, which in many ways were in advance of Europe technologically up to about the fifteenth century. The long, slow, steady rise in the folk technology of Europe after the fall of Rome, as represented, for instance, in the use of the stirrup and the horse collar, the iron shod plow, the waterwheel, the beveled gear, and somewhat later the compass, the windmill, and printing, owed a great deal to the slow movement of technology, mainly overland from China. A visitor from outer space looking at the world in, let us say, about the year 1000 would certainly have identified China as the "middle kingdom" in terms of technology, with an outer crescent of somewhat similar development in Islam, and would have seen Europe as a somewhat undeveloped penninsula, rather on the edge of the civilized world, although advancing rapidly. Nevertheless, it was Europe of the Renaissance out of which organized science developed, not out of Islam or China or the isolated cultures of America and Africa.

The Christian milieu of Europe, coupled perhaps with the rediscovery of Greek thought after the fall of Constantinople and the contacts with Islam, had something to do with the rise of science. Christianity legitimated both manual labor (*laborare est orare*—to work is to pray) and the reality of the material world in the Incarnation. A religion born in a stable, founded by a carpenter, propagated by a fisherman and a tent maker, was much closer to the material world than the speculations of Indian philosophers or the cultivation of Confucian gentlemanliness. This sense of the importance and reality of the material world is perhaps something that comes originally from the Jews. Jehovah is first and foremost a craftsman and a rewarder of faithful work. The three great Jewish religions—Christianity, Islam, and Marxism—are all much more materialistic than the esoteric religions of India, which tend to regard the material world as an illusion, something to be escaped from, whether in Hinduism or in Buddhism. It is interesting that Shinto is also a rather materialistic religion, promising good things in this life, which perhaps may account for the fact that Japan found it so easy to enter the modern world. Even in China, it might be argued, the working-class religions never made it to the top, as Christianity did with Constantine, and therefore Confucianism, while it was worldly enough, did not encourage innovation.

Another possible reason why science originated in Europe was that Europe had about the optimum degree of political disorganization. In the first place it had a long tradition of separation of church and state, as between the Pope and the Emperor. Furthermore, Europe had about the optimum degree of political disunity. China was a little too well organized for evolution. Evolution takes place in ecosystems, not in organisms. The price of unity is always death. Europe was more like an ecosystem, with its diverse principalities and its loose power structure and the innumerable cracks in the system. It is usually in the cracks of the system that mutation can take place and survive. China was too well organized with its mandarins and had too few cracks, and also had an upper class which despised manual labor. Consequently, the enormous inventiveness of the Chinese tended to go off into toys, like the south-pointing carriage.

Mutation is always heresy. If successful, it is a threat to the comfortable equilibrium of the existing climactic ecosystem. When successful, of course, it becomes another orthodoxy. A too powerful orthodoxy can suppress heresy and hence suppress mutation. Where there are rival orthodoxies, however, mutation has a better chance. Europe had many states and principalities, and after the Reformation it had many centers of spiritual power. Copernicus got away with it probably because Poland was a long way from Rome. Poor Bruno, of course, did not get away with it. Galileo got away with it under his breath. Then the cat was out of the bag. Kepler, and to some extent Newton, lived in the two worlds of religion and science. Almost the first scientist who was openly agnostic was Laplace. Priestley at least was a Unitarian minister and Dalton a Quaker. Adam Smith was something more than a deist. Darwin was certainly an agnostic, although Mrs. Darwin was a devout member of the Church of England. Marx might almost be called a devout atheist. He reacted very strongly against, but never really escaped, his Lutheran upbringing.

Another aspect of the scientific subculture which ties in with both its Christian and its European origins is its very unusual and remarkable ethos. The scientific community puts a very high value on curiosity, veracity, testing, and stresses persuasion by evidence and not by threat. Neither folk cultures nor politically powerful orthodoxies lay much stress on curiosity. "Curiosity killed the cat" is an old English proverb. Too much curiosity can get you into trouble in almost any folk culture. And powerful people seldom like people being curious about what they do. This is noticeable even in the United States, which has a strong official culture of openness and a Freedom of Information Act. Veracity is a cardinal virtue in the scientific community, violation of which is almost the only thing that can lead to excommunication. A scientist caught out in falsifying his results can never hold his head up again.

The ethic of testing is by no means unknown in folk cultures, as evidenced, again, by proverbs—"the proof of the pudding is in the eating." Democratic institutions no doubt represent highly imperfect mechanisms for the testing of political authority and political decision. Testing, however, is a paramount virtue in the scientific community. An untested, and still more an untestable hypothesis is to be regarded at best with amused condescension, at worst with total rejection, though there may not always be agreements as to what constitutes a satisfactory test.

A fourth characteristic of the scientific ethos, that people should be persuaded only by evidence and never by threat, is again somewhat unusual. It is not always practiced in graduate schools, where nonconformity beyond a certain limit of tolerance may be treated by expulsion, or at least by low grades. But among scientific peers the taboo is virtually unbreakable.

It could certainly be argued that all four elements of the scientific ethic are implicit in the New Testament: veracity even to the point of a taboo on oaths, curiosity about truth, testing to the point of challenge of received authority, and a repudiation of threat in the Cross. In the Christian tradition it is found most clearly perhaps in those groups that have stressed the conduct of individual life according to what they saw as the New Testament ethic, like the Franciscans in Catholicism, and the Moravian, Mennonite, Quaker, and Brethren variants of Protestantism.

The scientific ethic, however, may also have roots in European law, especially perhaps in the Germanic tradition, which reaches its fruition in the English Common Law. Here, also, there is a high value on curiosity, on what really happened; on veracity, to tell the truth and nothing but the truth; on testing, with the low value which is placed on hearsay evidence and on the principle that the judge should be persuaded only by the evidence presented in the court and should under no circumstances be influenced by threat or by bribery. It is hardly necessary to say that these principles are by no means necessarily always fulfilled in practice, but they have remained as ideals of the law for a long time and the ethic of the scientific community undoubtedly owes something to this tradition. Aspects of the tradition are also found in Roman law, but they are much less common in the legal systems of Eastern countries, where rulers have been much less checked in their arbitrariness by a code of legal conduct and individual rights before the law. How much the legal ethic and the Christian ethic in Europe owe to each other I do not know. This would make an extremely interesting subject for historical research.

The rise of science has continually led to a challenge to existing religious ideas and often has led to very serious conflict between science and religion, both within the noosphere, in the "ecosystem" of competing ideas and images of the universe, and also in the realm of organization and politics, beginning, of course, with Bruno and Galileo. Protestantism, at least in its post-Lutheran phases, was perhaps more friendly to science, but even here the substitution of the authority of the Bible for that of the church and the hierarchy easily led to conflict, as we see in the Scopes trial in Tennessee and in the creationists' political activity today. Marxism in its political–religious aspects, while officially claiming to be "scientific," in fact has occasionally been highly hostile to science, as in the famous Lysenko dispute in the Soviet Union and the virtual extermination of genetics there and indeed of some geneticists. To find a parallel indeed to this fierce persecution of a legitimate branch of science as a heresy we would have to go back to Bruno and Galileo. It is ironic indeed that Marxism, with its pretentions to scientific rationality, should have produced so many examples of a cult of personality totally inconsistent with any aspect of the ethic of science, and more extreme than any "Caesaropapism" into which the Christian Church may have fallen.

Outside the Soviet Union the scientific community has rarely, if ever, invoked political power to enforce conformity, except insofar as it has gotten involved with the military and has hence been forced to adopt conditions of secrecy and the exclusion of "politically unreliable" characters. In a more subtle form, however, the scientific community has often exercised a strong taboo on interests and forms of communication which do not conform to its subculture. There is nothing peculiar about this—all subcultures do it—and to some extent this problem is resolved by a process of separation of roles. There is a kind of tacit agreement in the scientific community that what the scientist does on Sunday or in the privacy of his home is nobody's business but his own, as long as he doesn't talk about it when he gets among his fellow scientists. This same taboo may apply to politics as it does to religion. These are regarded as unsavory fields of discourse in the professional and indeed in the business community. In our day indeed the relations between science and religion might well be described under the heading "peaceful coexistence." This, however, may well be achieved at the cost of having the boundary between them become something of a no man's land or a Berlin Wall. In this no man's land of the noosphere, however, some very interesting things grow, and a few foolhardy souls may be tempted to explore it.

One is somewhat tempted to invoke the right-brain versus left-brain hypothesis and to look at science as primarily a left-brain activity and religion as a right-brain activity. This, however, like all dichotomies, is a bit too simple. The role of religious experience at many different levels, from the comfortable feeling of the churchgoer or the communicant to the ecstasies of the mystic, is well documented and certainly a good deal of it comes out of the right brain. Nevertheless, it has an orderliness and a unity of its own, and is subject to the analytical procedures which are supposed to be characteristic of the left brain. Theology comes as much out of the left brain as does science.

Even science, however, has a strong right-brain element in it, particularly in the formation of theories and concepts, which has some elements of the mystical about it. Scientific theory might well be described as testable fantasy about the real world. The testing may be a little humdrum, but the fantasy from quarks to quasars is by no means wholly divorced from the religious imagination. Even mathematical discovery has a certain mystical quality about it. The working out of the implication of old theories may be solid, left-brain logic, but the leap of the imagination which produced the differential calculus or analytical geometry, or even the theory of fuzzy sets, is an intuitive leap on the part of the discoverer, which pretty clearly owes a lot to the right brain.

Teilhard's extraordinary vision of the universe evolving from Alpha to Omega had a remarkable quality of combining the scientific with the religious vision, as well as did his vision of the continual ongoing drive and prejudice of the evolutionary process toward what we should not be ashamed to call "truth" and "goodness." His vision of an evolutionary drive was remarkably akin to that of the Holy Spirit, as a process continually at work in the minds and hearts of the human race, or of George Fox's inward light that continually "revealed sin and drew us out of it."

Conflict arises when what science regards as evidence, religion erects as indubitable truth. The view that the Bible, or the Pope, or the Koran, or any other source of revelation is infallible is uncongenial to the scientific culture and is a potential source of conflict. This does not mean that authority cannot be treated with respect, but for the scientist the only ultimate authority is the real world which he is investigating, and which speaks to him through testing, but always through fallible human minds. There is an inevitable tension here between science and faith; it should neither be denied nor should it be unduly feared, for it can be very creative. Nevertheless, it can also be agonizing. No one has expressed this any better than Tennyson in "In Memoriam," all the more remarkable because it came almost a whole generation before Darwin:

> The wish, that of the living whole
> No life may fail beyond the grave,
> Derives it not from what we have
> The likest God within the soul?
>
> Are God and Nature then at strife,
> That Nature lends such evil dreams?
> So careful of the type she seems,
> So careless of the single life,
>
> That I, considering everywhere
> Her secret meaning in her deeds,
> And finding that of fifty seeds
> She often brings but one to bear,
>
> I falter where I firmly trod,
> And falling with my weight of cares
> Upon the great world's altar-stairs
> That slope thro' darkness up to God,
>
> I stretch lame hands of faith, and grope,
> And gather dust and chaff, and call

To what I feel is Lord of all,
And faintly trust the larger hope.

"So careful of the type?" but no.
From scarped cliff and quarried stone
She cries, "A thousand types are gone;
I care for nothing, all shall go.

Thou makest thine appeal to me.
I bring to life, I bring to death;
The spirit does but mean the breath:
I know no more." And he, shall he,

Man, her last work, who seem'd so fair,
Such splendid purpose in his eyes,
Who roll'd the psalm to wintry skies,
Who built him fanes of fruitless prayer,

Who trusted God was love indeed
And love Creation's final law—
Tho' Nature, red in tooth and claw
With ravine, shriek'd against his creed—

Who loved, who suffer'd countless ills,
Who battled for the True, the Just,
Be blown about the desert dust,
Or seal'd within the iron hills?

No more? A monster then, a dream,
A discord. Dragons of the prime,
That tare each other in their slime,
Were mellow music match'd with him.

O life as futile, then, as frail!
O for thy voice to soothe and bless!
What hope of answer, or redress?
Behind the veil, behind the veil.*

Science is deeply upsetting to the traditional metaphors and image of religion. The cozy three-storied world of Dante with hell underground, purgatory at the south pole, heaven beyond the last sphere of the stars that surround us, with God ruling over all, and the consoling drama of Creation, Fall, and Salvation have all been blown into a cold, frightening universe, inconceivably vast in both time and space, in which we are only an infinitesimal speck. It is no wonder that the church was deeply worried by Galileo and that Darwin in many ways is even more worrying. Nevertheless, science too is in a deep moral crisis because of the enormous increase in the power which it has given the human race, both for good and ill, and even for its own destruction. Furthermore, science is a partial, not a complete culture; the scientist has only partial identity. The ideas of science, magnificent as they are, have produced nothing like Chartres or Handel's Messiah, or Dostoyevsky's novels.

The vertical thrust of religion toward the ultimate and the ineffable, and the horizontal thrust of science toward the ordinary, the comprehensible, and the testable, indeed, form a cross, which those of us who have experienced both must bear throughout our lives. There is no doubt that Teilhard de Chardin bore it bravely and well.

NOTES

*Stanzas LV and LVI.

SUMMARY OF RESPONSE AND DISCUSSION

Dr. Monika Hellwig told of Teilhard's Christian faith legitimating his science. It gave such radical coherence to what he was doing that it liberated him for his creative vision. She then commented on the hostility of science and religion.

> Theologians of my age and vintage are doing an awful lot of penance for the theologians who preceded us. There was a day when the theologians bullied the scientists quite mercilessly. Now I think that it has turned the other way around; today the scientists are getting back. I hope the day will come when there is a partnership among equals of two very mature disciplines.

An intervention from the floor told of scholars in China and Japan from the twelfth century onwards having a great interest in the investigation of external things; this interest was related to their Neo-Confucian thought. Boulding responded that the Chinese knew an enormous amount of natural history, but natural history is not science. Science must have the correct taxonomies; this the Chinese did not have e.g.: they did not know the periodic table. Boulding told of Joseph Needham writing twelve volumes on the history of Chinese science and confessing that he still did not know why science had not begun there.

Prigogine told of the Jesuits bringing Newtonian science to China. But the Chinese "considered the idea that there are laws to nature more or less ridiculous." They saw nature as a whirlwind. But today, when science is taking on more qualitative features, its message has become much more universal. Prigogine suggested that the opposition between science and religion had developed "because each one of them claimed to know the truth; the only problem each of them had was how to transmit that truth." Newtonians (and even Newtonians modified by quantum and relativity effects) believed that the truth was there. This is precisely what we have begun to doubt. "I think we are all coming to agree that the universe is much stranger than we could have thought or imagined."

A psychologist from the audience told of scientific creativity involving a nonrational process and asked if therefore it could be considered a new form of prayer or meditation. Hellwig responded that prayer has taken many forms. But in any form—

it does invite a larger view, a quieter view, a slower moving view, and, therefore, a less constrained view of reality. Therefore, I would say that it could be very closely related to the kind of creativity that we wish to awaken in the sciences.

6

Teilhard and the Esthetic

Paolo Soleri

Is there a Teilhardian esthetic? My thesis is that there is, provided
the esthetic is the real aim of a reality in the process of creating itself. A
"beautiful" divinity is not unheard of. Can semantics propose destiny,
an escatological consummation?

As a category in the conscious world, the esthetic has been annoy-
ingly unruly from time immemorial. It does not fit most of the respect-
able models of reality. Sniping at it from the other disciplines, science,
philosophy, religion helps little. It manages to survive as the *enfant ter-
rible*; to my perception it is the *enfant* destined to embrace all and metamorphosize all and I mean all of reality, the cosmos.

At times, one goes on the assumption that beauty is an attribute of
divinity and that consequently the religious person is a seeker of beauty.
Facts do not seem to bear out such rationale. Quite often the religious
person speaks of the beauty of the soul and the beauty of grace.[1] He
means that piety, love, compassion and the divinities themselves, are
beautiful. One could then ask is God loving, compassionate, graceful,
because it is beautiful? Or is beauty defined as love, compassion, grace?
Or is beauty some sort of ambiguous, now you see it, now you don't,
shroud? Or is it a modulation floating among things, objects, beings, actions? Is beauty a category or an additive one can stir into morals,
prayers, political actions, social commitments, compassionate respons-
es, love, etc.?

My contention is that God and all its attributes is but an aesthetic manifestation. That is, the aim of all things is not God but beauty. That is to say the groping of reality is toward the beautiful and divinity is an attribute of it. Or to make a shocking example, it is not that the artist is an instrument for the glorification of church and God but that the religious institutions and the simulations called God are at the service of the beauty that the artist tries to create. That is, the evolutionary–cosmic process is an esthetogenesis. Esthetogenesis comprehends but is not comprehended by compassion, grace, equity, knowledge, perfection. All those are instrumental to its genesis.[2]

This is not a new proposition but it might well be still a radical or an heretical one and it needs clarification to say the least.

I do not pretend to do so but I will, hopefully with some coherence, make some point in favor of the proposition. I will do so by pulling Omega into the picture: My "definition" of Omega is somewhat different than Teilhard's. I see Omega as a hypothesis worth working for, because it is the hypothesis that perhaps proposes the only possible achievements of perfection. A totality that is all comprehensive in time and space and as such is equitable and by its creational genesis, is esthetic. As a genesis and as a totality it suggests that Omega is the seed of the cosmos, a seed which generates from the endless metamorphosis of evolution. As a seed it is the genetic matrix of its creator (evolution) and the trigger for resurrection. Since a seed is in a way the resurrection of the parent, the ultimate seed, at the end of time, is the resurrection of all reality.

Wo-man's mind has struggled for thousands of years trying to rationalize the esthetic. All definitions are untrue inasmuch as truth demands completeness and completeness is not of this world (but of the world to come of which this world will be a part). But if definitions are untrue, they are not useless or mindless. They reflect the environment from which they originate, or they reflect the response or reaction to the environment of which they were part.

I propose the divine as the prerogative of the infinitely beautiful. In fact, at the end of the tunnel of time it will be impossible to distinguish the beautiful from the graceful, from the equitable, the lovable, the harmonious. Omega will be all of them (or will be a deception) and all of them form the concluding act of esthetogenesis, the creation of the Omega seed of the cosmos (reality becoming), that is, Omega *will be* all of them or it will not be.

There is then a provisional kind of beauty, as there is a provisional kind of grace, a provisional kind of equity, etc. Inasmuch as they are "perfectible" *they are not perfect.* Then for instance an imperfect equity contains the denial of itself. Inequity is part of the perfectible equity. The only equitable equity is the equity not available yet to reality, therefore reality is inequitable. Would that mean that Lake Michigan is black because it contains a drop of India ink? Yes, in a sense there is blackness in the Lake even if it amounts to one drop of black ink. Perfection is exactly what the blackened lake is not in the sense of water not adulterated by ink. It is also quite clear that the inequity of reality amounts to tankers full of black ink in the lake of a reality made of pasts creating the future via the endless run of present after present.

In this endless process the seeking of equity and justice comes about with the appearance of wo-man's mind to engross the earlier version of them: Fitness and justness. The human mind (-body) cannot find satisfaction in fitness. It must seek equity and compassion. It cannot find satisfaction in justness. It must seek justice and love. Reality is impervious to such "transcendence" (see the foodchain mandate of eat or be eaten). Therefore, (A) the mind invents that which embodies equity, compassion, justice, love. It calls it God. (B) Wo-man "depicts" divinity via the esthetic, not only via subject matter (the crucifixion for instance) but by stance. Therefrom, my definition of esthetic:

Given a reality which is intrinsically unknowable and which development, evolution, is intrinsically inequitable the human soul is prey of an inextinguishable anguish impervious to the blandishment of science, medicine, psychology, religion, philosophy, politics, etc. The act that can to a certain degree transcend such reality and transform the inequitable is the esthetic act. As the unknowable and the equitable are transrational and transtemporal so it is the action that metamorphosizes them. Such esthetic action is more than an anticipation of perfection, grace, divinity, it is a splinter, a fragment of them. It is dust of divinity, a particle of the full, completed esthetogenesis.

In fact divinity is the end result of a (total) unification of all such esthetic dust into the esthetic genesis-denouement. Omega is *the* beautiful.

While art transforms matter, it is matter transfigured; religion seeks the transformation of matter by way of myth and prophecy.

Religion designs all sort of simulations of Omega. They fall constantly short of target. It could not be otherwise. We cannot even describe, simulate an existing dust particle of the esthetic because the esthetic "thing" is undescribable. How could we describe the summation of all beauty, the nonexistent beauty of the nonexistent Omega?

If the beautiful has its apogee in the full esthetogenetic process, metamorphosizing not sections of the cosmos but the cosmos in toto, the esthetic is fundamentally "manipulation" (metamorphosis).

Then what distinguishes technology, manipulation via science, and esthetic "manipulation" via anguish? The first is instrumental for the creation of the second which is the aim. The metamorphosis of "matter" into beauty–spirit.

Here is where a Teilhardian illumination of sorts could be proposed. As "matter" is not a burden but the media, the transformation–metamorphosis of matter is not expedient but substantial to the process of "divinization." Then if science might well be a dialogue between physicality and mind (Prigogine), something else, something more, has to go about besides dialogue if "spirit-God" is to eventually create itself. This something more is "manipulation," that is the technology of creating God via the metamorphosis of reality.

There are at least what I believe to be two good reasons for "manipulation" of matter. (1) As discrete demiurge we would not go along with a mountain of chipped away marble surrounding a puny statuette, the ring of entropy (disorder) surrounding the tiny bit of order that "has caused it." Therefore, for God's sake, let's at least prophesy that the whole of cosmos will "order" itself, no chip ignored, into grace. (2) Space, time, mass energy, our constituents if not our makers, are also our nemesis. In the presence of them, even a residual of them, full grace is not just improbable but impossible (see Science, Tao, Nirvana and the dualism they speak of). Only the total "manipulation" of matter into "spirit" will bring about grace, love, beauty in full.

Teilhard de Chardin could perhaps have proposed that independently from what the difference might be, love is the bond between esthetic and technology. Love unbound would see them coming together and coincide, into what? I propose into that which I called not Omega but Omega seed. Then under the banner of love we would move on the track of technology and on the track of esthetic or, perhaps better put, with love as the indispensable splicing of desirable technology and a *bona fide* esthetic, reality might slowly metamorphosize into Omega Seed.

If as the ever obliging martian I look down (or up or sideways) upon the hominids what do I see: Homo faber (technology), homo scientificus, homo estheticus, homo theologicus within the envelope of homo amantis (loving). The manipulators are homo faber and homo estheticus. Homo scientificus is the seeker of "truth" as such always turned to the past (the only reality), while homo theologicus, eternally fantasizing, is anticipating the loving one, God. If homo scientificus and homo theologicus get together they can develop a technology of knowledge that is both past rooted and future oriented. A lot of love must shower on them to lubricate the cogs and keep at minimum the heat of ignorance, intolerance, bigotry, self-deception and arrogance.

If homo technologicus and homo estheticus get together the theory of knowledge developed by homo scientificus and homo theologicus would afford larger and larger chunks of the material world to vivify and take conscience of itself. This is the animation of matter, slowly extending the esthetogenetic process throughout the cosmos.

If there is such a thing as a priestly mode it works at the simulation of perfection through the filter of the human limitations, mind included. It plays such a game by the (rear) mirror technique. What it sees in front, the future, it postulates to be the reflection of what it thinks to be in the back, the past. That keeps the priest prisoner of an anti-future, anti-time paradigm. It makes him the paradox of life denying life, in the name of life. A nearsighted engagement on a clear sighted need.

If there is such a thing as the scientific mode it works at the unveiling of truth as if truth were given (the priestly assumption). It plays the game of the solicitor that does not identify in the solicited any part of himself (classical physics). The scientist observes reality from a self that, according to his "reality," reality is the least concerned with.

If there were such a thing as the technocrat mode it would work at the manipulation of matter as if what matters were purely to make black that which is white then to make white that which was black. In a better kind of wrongness binge, it plays the game of digestor, not much asked about the input, even less asked about the output (in cosmic terms) so far as it sells at a profit.

If there is an esthetic mode it works on the creation of a world without residual means. A world that "at the end" is all sounds and songs and no instruments and that keeps the artist dwelling in deeper and deeper ambiguities that resolve the anguish of the moment by proposing a stronger one in its place.

Of the four, the technocratic mode is the most blind. It does what it does mostly for the wrong reasons (the consumerism utopia) but becomes in the process proficient at the magic of metamorphosis. This is not the only reason the esthetic finds the technological both appealing (indispensable) and impervious. It finds it difficult to pull it beyond the clinically functional (in the best of cases). It is also aware that both esthetic and technologic have propensities for extravagance, that which priests and scientists for their singular reasons abhor and rightly so. The consequences of extravagance are idiosyncratic displays on one side (see the glut of narcissism of contemporary "art") and the gadget syndrome on the other (see the shopping center).

For the artist the true vocation might be in seeking the universal that transfigures his personal suffering into the anguish of living, and then extracts from it that which transacts it into the esthetic.

For the technocrat–technologist the true vocation could be found in the realization that matter is wanting of consciousness, sensitivity, spirit, and that to metamorphosize it into beauty it takes a technology of grace. The technologist must become a techno-logian, the theologian of reality.

Immersed as we all are in all such modes at different degrees of dedication and belief, we are (individually) torn within ourselves and torn we are also from each other. Anxiety makes us ready for indictment, if as priests we feel subservient to the scientist, if scientist subservient to the technologist . . . and so on. This conflict is not limited to intelligentsia because we all, uneducated, educated, scholars, look for the focus of things, for that which will not go away, for a raison d'être. The art of living, as far from narcissism as from masochism, escapes us in almost monotonous refusals. It probably escaped Teilhard also, afflicted as he was, as he must have been, by the peculiar torment of seeing himself and the best of himself at that, refused by Mother Church. But perhaps fragment by fragment he lived esthetics even more than being consciously attentive to matters esthetic. In fact, the affliction was its true anguish and his work, more and more cause for the Church's refusal, more and more became the transcending of such anguish, and as such a fragment of esthetogenesis.

To obviate the inequitable by way of piety and compassion is not to act esthetically, it is to act altruistically. But altruism lives only in the shadow of inequity. Once inequity is extinguished, altruism is "out of work." Altriusm can exist only if "evil" exists. The esthetic is something else, it does not exist in function of something else. It is an end in itself. Perhaps it is *the* end.

What of love? If the esthetic were a fish, water would be love, the indispensable medium. The water turns out to be for the sake of the fish, not the fish for the sake of the water.

Is there then an esthetic Teilhard? And how large is its shadow? What there is of Teilhard esthetics is to be found in the conversion (acceptable or not) of religion into esthetics. If religiousness is ultimately the longing for the beautiful, that which transcends the intrinsic inequity of the real, then Teilhard was eminently involved in things esthetic.

As you can see this brief exposition is full of assumptions and presumptions. I would be glad to debate at least some of them.

NOTES

1. It is often hard to separate the esthetic pursuit from some of the most despicable actions. See the infatuation of National Socialism with Richard Wagner.

2. The esthetic is the compassionate beauty, the beauty textured within reality when and after it has been filtered and recreated by the anguish of mind.

SUMMARY OF RESPONSE AND
DISCUSSION

Dr. Soleri gave a slide presentation of the one–building city he is now constructing in Arizona. The discussion that followed concerned questions of practicality. Dr. L. Dean Price began his response by telling of hearing Teilhard speak at Berkeley in the early 1950s. Ten years later he recognized the same gentle eyes on the cover of THE PHENOMENON OF MAN. He studied Teilhard and taught him; upon reading Paolo Soleri he recognized that Soleri was dealing with the "folding-in" process of which Teilhard spoke. Price told of his admiration for the design of Soleri, but he saw the *Aesthetogenesis* of which Soleri spoke involving an absolute perfection apart from all inequities; in this way it reminded him of Augustine's *City of God* or More's *Utopia*. But at the same time it seemed too far apart "from the imperfections of the built environment." Soleri's city would seem to call for "perfect people" to make such an ideal "civilization in the desert work." Just as the Agape of the New Testament includes the ability to love the unlovable and thus discover the numinous meaning of love—so Beauty must embrace the given situation and what is not beautiful.

Leakey objected that Soleri's work was far removed from the needs of hundreds of millions of people who lack even a cement floor. Soleri said that he was aware of these problems and the purpose of his work was to

> encourage the young people who work with us to look into the question of frugality. We want them to see that there is only a weak connection between happiness and consumerism. What we are doing is prototyping. That is why it involves a simple technology. It is a technology that might begin to bridge the gap between the world of the very poor and the fantasy world of the very rich.

Someone from the floor asked about the social structure that would permit such a massive concentration of people. Soleri answered that today indeed people are spreading apart. Luxury apartments and suburbia tell of segregation and disintegration. They are "the opposite of what we are trying to do." Crowding together is no crime; it is a basic fact of biology. "Life is crowding by definition." We humans are at the head of this process of crowding.

Each one of you is an enormously complex association of billions of systems; each of you is an incredibly complex and crowded phenomenon.

Prigogine observed that Soleri's design would impose an enormous structure on the people who would live there. Soleri responded that New York, Washington and even a village are imposed structures.

Structure is not the problem; the problem is what kind of structure. The structure of a two dimensional habitat is incapable of serving the intensity of life we are developing, and rightly so. Eventually we will have to recognize the nature of the living and the conscious and do our best to find congruence between what we are, what we preach and what we do. Compassion and love are to be found there and nowhere else.

7

The End of History: The Threefold Structure of Human Time-Consciousness

R. Panikkar

The inquiry into contemporary events leads me to think that we are not only at the end of *an* historical period—as many analysts today would agree[1]—but that we are ending *the* historical period of Mankind, which is to say that we are *at the beginning of the end of the Myth of History.*[2] In order to catch a glimpse of what a post-historical myth may represent, I shall describe it in relation to prehistorical and historical consciousness. The main elements of a post-historical myth are already present—or else we could not speak of it intelligibly—but its contours have not yet emerged for most people.[3] These three forms of consciousness are all human. This is why I speak of three moments of human time-consciousness; or rather of the threefold structure of human time-consciousness.[4] These three moments should not be interpreted chronologically, i.e., as though they followed one after the other. They are qualitatively different and yet intertwined, coexisting in one way or another, in the human race and the human person as well. The nonhistorical type is very much alive today, and trans-historical consciousness is equally present in our times. They are three modes of consciousness which are neither mutually exclusive nor dialectically opposed, but *kairologically* related.[5] I mean by this word the qualitative aspect of human time which represents at once the dominance of one mode over the others, according to idiosyncrasies of all sorts, and a certain temporal sequence which accords with the unfolding of individual and, especially, collective life.

The question of vocabulary here is almost insurmountable. Each word has a home. It may have received some hospitality in other neighborhoods, but hardly a word today has international citizenship, let alone global validity. Speaking within the historical myth, history must be the central point of reference; therefore I have called these three periods nonhistorical, historical and trans-historical. But this is only a device to introduce the three mentioned moments. First of all, they are not periods in the mass media sense of the word, but rather in the more complex sense suggested by the etymology of the word *period:* ways around, or recurring ways of being human.[6] Secondly, I might have called them *past directed, future oriented* and *present centered* time–consciousnesses, but because most writers and readers of our so-called contemporary literate cultures live within the prevalent historical moment, I shall not deny history the importance it has. Granting history this centrality, the three moments might be called prehistorical, historical and post-historical. But this would not do justice to the a-historical moments. My preference would be to call them kairological, historical and secular.[7] But I shall remain with the compromise of nonhistorical, historical and trans-historical.[8]

There may be no more formidable problem than the problem of time.[9] We are speaking here of a threefold human time–consciousness. The difficulty in communicating what I would like to say lies in the fact that from each of these time–consciousnesses we tend to scan the entire temporal spectrum. Most of my readers, as already noted, will tend to comprehend any human temporality in historical categories. Prehistorical Man generally does not know how to read or write, or at least does not make much of it.[10] And trans-historical consciousness does not much feel the need of that skill. And yet, bear in mind, the three modes are not mutually exclusive. In each one of us there exist more or less latent forms of nonhistorical and trans-historical time–consciousness, although modern Man may "historicize" them when thinking about them in our rational and historically conscious parameters. Those moments for which we would have given our entire life, those artistic experiences that seem to be intemporal, the realms of life which open up in deep meditation, besides the peak and ecstatic experiences in the face of the mysteries of life, suffering and death, could be adduced as examples of human consciousnesses which are irreducible to historical consciousness.

These three moments not only form a triad in our own individual lives, they are also analogously present in the collective unfolding of human existence, although in any given culture and from a sociological viewpoint one of them may predominate over the others.[11] And because the lives of most book–writers and readers unfold in historical time, I will have somehow to pay tribute to it by using a presentation and a language still tainted with historical overtones, as the very words pre-, post-, and even non, para- and trans- "historical" betray.

The argument of this study is as follows: Man is a temporal being.[12] His experience of time has three focal points: the past, the future, and the present. The predominance of one or another of these focuses makes up the three kairological moments to which I have alluded. The development of all three time–experiences accounts for the maturity of the human being—phylogenetically and ontogenetically. When the past is the paradigm through which we experience time, we have the nonhistorical moment (memory and faith are central); when it is the future, historical consciousness prevails (the will and hope are predominant); and when past and future are lived in terms of the present, we share in the trans-historical experience of reality (the intellect and love become fundamental).[13]

These three moments in human consciousness correspond to three periods of human existence on Earth—in the indicated sense of the word period. We could even date these periods.

Until the invention of writing, Man could not project all his creations into the future; the past had the most powerful grip on him. Tradition was paramount. Time comes from a Beginning. *Mythos.*

With the invention of writing, human specialization becomes possible. Progress is a sacred word. Time marches forward. The future belongs to God and God to the future. *History.*

When Man split the atom, the seemingly indestructible elements on which the entire world rested showed their vulnerability. The human technological miracle has itself been fissioned. The atoms of all sorts (spiritual and intellectual as well) are no longer indestructible. The past is broken and the future collapses. The present is the only time left. And it is this experience that opens the door to the predominance of the *Mystical.*

Before the description of these three moments, a criteriological description will be helpful.

I. METHODOLOGICAL REFLECTION

1. *The Subject Matter: Man*

Let us be clear that these three moments of human consciousness do not mean three different objects of consciousness, i.e., three different ways of looking at the world, while the human subject remains unchallenged and so, unchanged. They represent rather three different modes of being human, precisely because consciousness defines Man. Man is that speaking animal which speaks because it has something to say, i.e., because it possesses a self-consciousness which makes it aware of its own consciousness. And because of this, it speaks. The human animal speaks, not because it is aware of things and actions (as other animals also are), but because it is aware of itself doing this. And to communicate its subjective (reflective) intentions, it needs words. I would call it a *speaking consciousness, śabdabrahman.*[14]

In other words, if Man is essentially self-conscious, how can we know what Man is without taking into account all that human beings have *understood* themselves to be? The "object" Man of the study of Man also embraces the "subject" Man who undertakes the study. But this Man is not only I or we, the investigators, it is everybody. Everyman.[15] The study of Man entails the study of what humans think of themselves. Is such an enterprise possible? Possible perhaps, provided we keep it all the while open and provisional, i.e., maintain the awareness that we do not have access to the universal range of human experience.[16]

As if this were not enough, another difficulty arises: Man reveals himself not only in thinking but also in doing. How then can such a study be accomplished without taking into account all that Man has done? In fact, actions are as much crystallizations or revelations of Man's understanding of himself and the universe as are his theoretical reflections.[17] Now in the West, since Aristotle at least, Man's actions have been divided into those that return for the perfection of the agent: activities like feeling and understanding; and those which are directed *ad extra* for the perfection of something else.[18] We do not refer to the former, the *poiesis,* but to the latter, the human *praxis.*[19] Human *praxis* reveals what Man is, just as much as does *theoria*. Humans think, and all their thinking belongs to what Man is, but humans also act and all their activity belongs to human nature as well, even if the meaning of those acts has not reached reflective consciousness.

The attempt to reach such theoretical awareness is the task of philosophy. The study of such *praxis* is History.[20] The unfolding of such events is *Geschichte.*[21] Both History and *Geschichte* belong to Anthropology. I understand Anthropology as the *telling* of what Man is. *Geschichte* tells us what Man is through his deeds. History tells us what Man is by the interpretation of his deeds. *Geschichte* offers the *praxis,* History the theory of Man's constructs—and both, obviously, in relation to human (historical) facts. But History also means that dimension of human consciousness which makes the study of human praxis meaningful. It is historical consciousness that undertakes the study of History, precisely because it is convinced of the revelatory character of such an enterprise.[22] The study of History will tell us what Man is, as long as we believe Man to be an historical being.[23] This is extremely important and has often been overlooked. History is what it claims to be, namely "magistra vitae," the revelation of what Man is, the "unfolding of human reason" and the like, insofar as Man believes himself an historical being. In short, History is History inasmuch as we are in or believe in the Myth of History. All this discourse would have no meaning were we not somewhat convinced that we are historical beings living in History as our proper world, as the proper environment of the fish is water.

What then does it mean, in this context, that the historical period is coming to an end? It does not mean that we cease to take an interest in human praxis. It does not mean that we jump altogether outside time and space. Historicity should not be confounded with temporality. The phrase means that man ceases to consider himself as *only* an historical being, or *the* historical being, *Dasein,* and by this very fact ceases to be a merely historical being.[24] It means that men begin to question whether the study, or knowledge, of what they do and think exhaustively reveals what they are and gives them the clue to life, happiness and/or truth.[25] It means that the fulfillment of human life is no longer seen exclusively, or even mainly, in the historical unfolding (individual or collective) but also, or rather, in transtemporal experiences (not atemporal but tempiternal), as I shall try to spell out.

We should insist on this for a moment. The peculiar nature of the human being also consists in the *who* that *thinks* and *does,* besides the *what* that is thought and done. This constitutes the fundamental distinction between the so-called "natural," i.e., "physical" sciences and philosophical anthropology, i.e., the "humanities." The former intend to know *objects* (however modified by and dependent on the investigator); the latter seek to understand *subjects* (even if incompletely covered by the investigation). When "Science" studies Man it wants to know the object Man: what Man *is*. When Philosophy (or should I say philosophical Philosophy, to distinguish it from a certain modern scientific Philosophy) takes aim at the same target, it wants to understand the subject Man: who Man *is* and even who I, a man, *am* and you, *are*. The epistemological paradigm of the Natural Sciences is: "S is P." It strives to find the P fitting to S. The epistemological paradigm of at least some Philosophy is: "What am I?" so that it may also answer "What you are," and be able to formulate "Who Man is."[26]

Our particular case still needs a second degree of sophistication. Our problem has to do with more than the well-known fact that the Humanities cannot be totally objectified—since individual viewpoints also belong to the "subject matter." It has to do as well with the fact that the particular human awareness of an entire group of cultures (the historical ones) is called into question. This is possible only if we recognize the validity of a truly trans-cultural invariant, which we can only extrinsically locate through a genuine cross-cultural approach to the ultimate problems of human awareness. We cannot deny *a priori* the possibility of another human *a priori*. But the burden of proof lies in our capacity to show that this genre of discourse also makes sense to us.

The trans-cultural is a kind of homeomorphic equivalent to what European philosophy since Kant has called the transcendental, i.e., that which, being an *a priori* condition of our understanding, is given in any reality we understand, but always in the very form in which we understand it. Similarly, the trans-cultural does not stand alone. There is nothing just trans-cultural since we are always in a certain culture, even if it is a new or nontraditional one. Yet the cross-cultural approach to reality opens us to the discernment of something—although obviously not a "thing in itself"—present in the different homeomorphic notions of different cultures. It is rather that which allows the cross-cultural correlations and makes us aware that we are dealing with a homeomorphic notion.[27]

We know, for instance, that *dharma* cannot be rendered just by "justice." It may also mean "religion," "righteousness," "duty," "right," "feature," "character," and have still many other meanings. Likewise, we know that "religion" is not only *dharma.* It is also "bhakti," *karma-nistha, niyama sādhana, pūja* and many other words, each of them covering only a part of the meaning of the original. The relation is not univocal, one to one. Now if we are familiar with these two worlds of "dharma" and "religion," we shall detect that the numerous English words standing for *dharma* have little or nothing in common with the English linguistic world, and yet they all express *dharma.* Something similar could be put the other way around regarding our example of "religion." When we detect that the former series are all *dharmic* words and the latter "religious" words, we approach the trans-cultural. For a correct interpretation we need a cross-cultural approach. We need to understand, for instance, what *dharma* means in the *Gītā* and be able to render that meaning in English, or what "religion" means in the Vulgate and be able to put it into Sanskrit. It is when we discover that the relation is not bi-univocal that we may be able to choose the appropriate word, taking into consideration the trans-cultural factor. Only when I know that *dharma* means all those words in English, "religion" all those words in Sanskrit and yet univocally none of them; only when I choose the right word because something has dawned upon me that finds its proper expression in the language into which I am translating, almost as a new creation; only then am I in touch with the trans-cultural; it is not *dharma,* or religion, or duty, or *pūja*—and yet it allows me to find the appropriate word. Generally this happens because we know the context and then find the proper word, but this only postpones the problem because the context also has to be known by means of words.[28] We are touching the problem of the experience before its expression. There is no experience without expression, and yet they are not the same.[29]

The case of time is paradigmatic here. We may have a cross-cultural understanding of time. Different cultures have different experiences and understanding of the human and cosmic rhythms. What I am attempting here is to group these cultures in larger units according to one particular fundamental feature, like this one of "time." Time has to do with past, present and future, with the flow of events, with change, movement and the like. Time has to do with living and with being. But all these realities are lived and experienced differently by different human traditions. A cross-cultural understanding will show the differences and the similarities. But it is only with an awareness of the trans-cultural character of time that we may be able to detect the three modes of human time–consciousness which we are about to elaborate here.

In order to prepare the way for an intelligible discourse, we shall have to disclose the parameters of our investigation.

2. *The Human Scale: The Astrological Rhythm*

Between the cosmic yardstick of a Teilhard de Chardin, comprising hundreds of thousands of years, on the one hand, and the journalistic vision of just days or weeks, the sociological perspective of decades, or the historical angle of some centuries, on the other, lies the astrological meter of the Earth's rhythm.[30] This is the natural equinoctial rhythm of the Earth around the Sun, which takes 25,000 years for its axis to process round to the same alignment. This is the so-called Platonic or cosmic year. Each astrological month would then last 2,100 years. If we entered the period of Aquarius around 1950, ending the month of Pisces which began circa 150 B.C. my own perspective would be to situate the following reflections against the backdrop of the beginnings of what we call human history, which coincides with the two previous periods, i.e., Aries, from about 2250 B.C. and Taurus, which began around the year 4350 B.C.[31] Human history thus has a memory of roughly 6,000 years.[32] Can we say something meaningful on this scale?

I would like to venture some ideas, based not on astrological considerations, important as these are, but on my own diachronical and diatopical experiences of cultures and peoples we know.[33]

All the different rhythms are legitimate. The individual's needs for food cannot be dealt with on a yearly or even weekly basis; it is a daily concern. Politics cannot bypass or ignore the situation of the generation actually living within the *polis*. Historians have a wider span, natural scientists another, and philosophers would tend to further enlarge their perspective and somehow generate theories or opinions *sub specie aeternitatis*, or at least *in mundo sublunari*, i.e., valid for the human condition as such—Sociology of Knowledge notwithstanding.

Yet there is an intermediate span which has all too often been neglected, because it needs different scales and yardsticks.[34] There are problems too small to be measured by physical or biological laws, and too big to be treated in merely sociological categories. This is what I call the astrological scale. This scale is precisely defined by the magnitude of those phenomena which relate to Man as *homo sapiens* and to the solar system within the more comprehensive rhythms of our galactic system.

I should not be misunderstood. What has been said should not be interpreted in historical categories, as if we were speaking of the human historical clock measured in astronomical units. I am speaking not so much about a Newtonian or Einsteinian solar system, but about Man. The human scale is not just a larger meter than the historical one, but that meter capable of measuring the changes in human time–consciousness. It is not our time perception that is at stake here, but our own temporal being, which has in the last centuries of Western civilization all too often (though not always) been identified with historical being.

The true yardstick here is human language. It is somewhat disturbing to see human problems approached with superhuman paradigms like those of the astronomical and biological cycles. But it is equally unsatisfactory to tackle issues regarding Man and the nature of reality as experienced by the human being with limited calipers valid only for much more restricted phenomena. If the danger of the former is vagueness, from lack of concrete data, the latter approach runs the risk of oversimplification by unwarranted extrapolation.

Historical studies have to limit themselves to written documents and prehistorical research concentrates on human tools. Language, I submit, is the human *metron* par excellence. It measures the *humanum,* and it is more than just a tool or a document. It is human nature incarnated. Not only has the Logos become flesh; the flesh also becomes Logos. In language we have the crystallization of human experience and its tradition.[35] Human language is not a mere record of the past. It bears witness to human nature in the present. We should learn not only to decipher past documents, but also to read language.

And here the wisdom of prehistorical Man, as well as the teachings of the great masters of the historical period—perceived in a cross-cultural light—come to our aid without our having to escape into superhuman or metacosmic utopias. They have all paid the utmost attention to language. Teilhard de Chardin and Hindu Cosmology may be true in their contexts, but just as we should avoid using centimeters and seconds to evaluate our present human situation, we should equally eschew using light-years for human measurements.[36] The destiny of the human race cannot be judged only from the White House or the Kremlin, but also not exclusively from Mount Wilson, the Sri Aurobindo Ashram or a biological laboratory. Our scale is neither that of the United States presidential elections nor that of the zoo–biological species.[37] I am taking into account human consciousness of the last 20,000 at least, and human memory of the 6,000 elapsed historical years, in order to project our reflections into the coming millennia.[38] It is within this middle range that the human scale may be preserved. And it is here that the trans-historical consciousness may shed some light on the excruciating predicament of our times.[39]

3. The Crossing of the Human Ways: A Threefold Typology

It is the diachronical character of the contemporary scene, together with a proper cross-cultural methodology, which makes our enterprise here possible. We do not need to travel thousands of years back in order to find a nonhistorical experience of reality. It may suffice to travel perhaps some thousands of miles at most, but for many only some few yards beyond their habitats. We live in a diachronical world. We are contemporaries of the stone age people, the paleolithic peoples, the confucian sages, vedāntic pandits, renaissance women and electronic engineers. As to the cross-cultural sensitivities aroused here, many of the people aware of this problematic today are equally conscious that a single culture or a single way of thinking simply cannot do justice to the contemporary human situation. If we succeed in entering into nonhistorical human consciousness and also in detecting glimpses of the trans-historical, we may be able to describe in an intelligible manner the breakdown of the historical myth which we perceive to be occurring in our midst.

I should repeat that this threefold typology does not represent three watertight isolated compartments. In each human being and in each culture there lie more or less dormant the other two less predominant types. This, among other factors, is what makes for the irreducibility of human life, even on a theoretical level, to purely logical or rational parameters. In an overcondensed way I may describe this typology as follows:

When we say and believe: "The origins of humankind and/or of the Earth are in a heterogenous principle—i.e., in a transcendent point which has no direct connection with our present situation, although it explains it—this principle has to be the most important factor of reality, but we cannot properly know it, or direct it. We can at most entreat it. God is one name for such a principle, but by whatever name there it is: sovereign, inscrutable and transcendent. Although ever-present, this principle was at the origin of everything, the very source. The past then must be the most important category. Thus tradition is paramount. We have to find our way across this middle world, the *antarikṣa;*" when we respond positively to such a set of ideas, then we are in a nonhistorical frame of mind. The criterion of truth is what was and ever shall be. Authority is spontaneously recognized as an essential element in the order of reality. Memory is power.

When we say and believe: "In the Beginning was a specific Act of the God, an actually spoken Word of the Divine, a Birth of the God or the Hero—or the Foundation of the City, the Constitution, the Event, the datable Big Bang—this Beginning is important, it is indeed the beginning, but we must continue it, we must take life in our own hands and construct the future. Destiny does not depend on the whims of the Gods but on us, our behavior, and our thoughts as well. The future is the relevant category. Thus freedom is paramount; we are marching towards an eschatology which is the fruit of our deeds;" when we respond positively to such a set of ideas, then we are in an historical world. The criterion of truth is evidence of the fact, and fact is something which strikes our mind and compels it because of its unmistakable and undeniable spatio–temporal parameters. Creativity is spontaneously recognized as an essential element in the order of reality. To measure (distances to the Beginning and in between and to the Goal) is to think. This measuring is knowledge, and brings power.

When we say and believe: "There was neither Principle nor Event at the Beginning; each moment is its own beginning and end; to discharge on the past the burden of the present or to postpone for the future what we cannot deal with now is the greatest temptation on Earth; the present is the most important factor of reality because only the present has full ontological weight, as it were; life is neither a second edition of a heavenly paradigm nor a project projected into a more or less ideal future, neither a reminiscence nor a trial, nor a mission, nor capital which will yield interest; we have to pierce the crust of shallow temporality in order to find the core of it all, and thus happiness;" when we respond positively to such a set of ideas, then we are in a trans-historical mentality. The criterion of truth is the personal experience about which there can be no doubt. Freedom is spontaneously recognized as the most essential element of reality. To have insight into, i.e., to realize the nature of things, brings power.

It should be noted that we are dealing here with fundamental attitudes toward reality. From the platform of one attitude we are entitled to say that we do not understand the other one or that we do not agree with it, but this does not cancel the fact of those other basic human experiences. And the fact that they are human makes them part and parcel of how Man has understood himself to be, and thus of what Man is.

To put the same thing differently: cross-cultural studies do not deal only or even mainly with how "we" (with our categories and from our perspective) understand "others" but with how others have understood themselves in a way which we may also come to understand or at least surmise—because the encounter with the other has not only enlarged our field of vision but also changed our own stance. It is certainly legitimate that from a certain point of view, for instance that of modern science, we try to understand the totality of the real and that we declare ourselves ready to change our own parameters, should the "object" of our investigation so require. Every worldview has an inbuilt and legitimate claim to truth and thus to universality. Nobody can from the outside dictate the flexibility of any mode of knowledge or way of life.[40] This is what makes dialogue possible and fruitful. But there are patterns of intelligibility, metaphysical options, basic attitudes and/or fundamental human perspectives which seem to be mutually incompatible, sometimes incomprehensible or even wrong, and yet are nevertheless represented in the human panorama. This is what makes for the seriousness of pluralism, as we are still going to see.[41] It is not the object of science, in our example, which is not universal, but the scientific perspective. Science is one way of looking at and thus being in the world, but not the only possible way—indeed. We are dealing here with something more fundamental than different ways of thinking.[42] We are dealing with different possible ways of being human—all of them connected, however, in and with the *dia-logos.*[43]

Be this as it may, it is this set of human perceptions of reality, including the reality of Man, which entitles us to cross the historical frontier and speak of a trans-historical human consciousness, already kairologically present in the prevalent historical consciousness of contemporary Western Man.

II. NONHISTORICAL CONSCIOUSNESS

Nonhistorical consciousness informs the prevalent worldview and self-understanding of so-called prehistoric Man, from time immemorial up until the commonly accepted beginning of the historical period of humankind. This does not mean, however, that prehistoric Man belongs only to the chronological prehistoric past. Nonhistorical consciousness is a contemporary kairological reality, not only for the so-called "primitive," but also for the modern cosmopolitan dweller. One of the reasons why I propose to call the religiousness of these cultures *primordial* is because they represent something primordial in every human being. This nonhistorical time–awareness, which fosters a vision of life and thus of reality different from the historical vision, is one example.

The decisive break is the invention and spread of writing. That old Egyptian legend related by Plato of the king berating his fellow-God for having invented Script represents this mutation.[44] With the invention of Script, past events acquire a consistency of their own without the need of personal involvement; they may become (external) reminders without being (internal) memories. They are simply written down in some archives. From this moment forward, your life can be encoded not only in your memory and your flesh but in external devices (the writings) which can bear witness for or against you and vouch for events which are—because you have perhaps forgotten them—not entirely real to you. Past events acquire independent reality. They can be stored, frozen, so to speak, fossilized in special devices of clay, stone, leaves or artificial materials. They do not need to be accumulated in Man's memory and to permeate the present. But they can be brought back to mind by the political leader or resurrected by the prophet, for they are still encoded in Man's brain and language. Above all, they can be projected into the future by accumulation of the experience of past generations. We may recall that a Mediterranean city, Byblos, became famous for its parchment, and some Mediterranean religions have become even more famous for calling the "Bible" their cornerstone. Historical consciousness emerges, as it were, from a more general nonhistorical consciousness and gathers power with the invention of human Script. With this, time acquires a certain independence in regard to Man. The human being will have to reconquer time, and henceforward sets out in search of time lost or time to come.

Prehistorical Man, on the contrary, lives mainly in *space*. Time is subsidiary to space. An autonomous (human) time is not of much import for his consciousness. Time is cosmic, or rather anthropocosmic, for the separation of the cosmic and the human is not (yet) made. In other words, time is natural, not cultural. The seasons of the Earth measure time, not the exploits of Man, as in historical eras.[45] The human beings are agriculturalists and/or hunters, settlers and/or nomads. Biological or vital functions, in the noblest but also most elementary sense of the word, occupy their minds and hearts: human attention is concentrated on birth, puberty, marriage, death, eating, playing, dreaming and also, I would assume very importantly, on speaking. Work is done in order to eat, drink, and be protected by clothing and a house.

But we must not forget that to eat, drink, sleep, mate and so on are all theocosmic and not just "biological" acts. Work is done primarily for the living, for life to go on from the ancestors to their descendants, for the world to continue. But living means "to walk in Beauty," as the Navajo would say, to enjoy life, to be open to the beauty of nature, the joy of human intercourse on all levels, the ecstasy of self-discovery and the complex numinous relationships with supernatural and superhuman powers. Men go to war to rescue a woman, to wreak vengeance, to obtain better hunting or ploughing grounds, or perhaps also to humiliate their neighbors, or eventually even to conquer an empty space, but they do not march into the *future*. What would it mean to them? That is left to the Alexanders, Akbars, and Napoleons of the historical period.

The World of prehistorical Man, his environment (*circumstantia, Umwelt*) is the *theocosmos:* the divinized universe. It is not a "world of Men" but neither is it the "world of Gods" as a separate and superior realm hovering over the human. Man shares the world with the Gods. He still drinks Soma with the Gods.[46] The Gods do not yet form a clan of their own, as they will do when history is about to begin. It is the world of history that views the prehistorical world as "full of Gods."[47] This is a vision from the outside. In the nonhistorical consciousness, it is the world itself that is divinized, or rather divine. The divine permeates the cosmos. The forces of nature are all divine. Nature is "supernatural," so to say. Or rather, nature is that which is being "natured," born—from or of the divine. Prehistorical Man's home, his background, is a cosmotheological one. Harmony is the supreme principle—which does not mean that it has been achieved. The meaning of life consists both in entering into harmony with nature and in enhancing it.[48]

Prehistorical Man certainly has clear ideas of past, present and future. The mother may worry about her children or the grandfather about his crops, as do historical human beings. But their time is not, I submit, historical; i.e., it is not centered on Man as an accumulation of the past with which to build "historical reality." What is not assimilated or not desired is discarded.[49] Time is not there to build a society or to create a better future. You are not the owner but the "enjoyer" of your time. Time is the day or the night. Time is an old man or God, a gift of the past. It is the rhythm of nature, not the construct of culture. One tribe may want to overpower another, to have better or larger pastures, but the idea of an Empire, a Kingdom, a Church, a collective enterprise different from what nature does or separated from the rhythms of the cosmos, makes no sense to prehistorical Man.[50] The meaning of life does not consist in building a Great Society on Earth, a powerful organization, but rather in enjoying life in the best possible way.[51] Prehistorical Man cannot believe, for instance, that a powerful State will enhance the value of the lives of its individuals.[52] Eschatology coincides with the end of one's own life.[53] You begin every day anew. Each day has enough of its own weight.[54]

This nonhistorical consciousness could also be called the *pre-scriptural mentality*. It is difficult for an historical mentality to imagine life without scripture. Nonhistorical consciousness entrusts everything to memory—not to reminders. The past is present only insofar as memory and the patterns of daily life preserve it. The presence of the past is in the living of it, in every detail of life. The legends are in the telling, just as there is no song until it is sung. Accumulation of knowledge is possible only to the extent to which one can digest it. Food can be gathered in silos but knowledge has to be actualized and memory is the only treasure house. Tradition is the very life of the present. The sense of life does not lie in what I still have to live, but in what I have already lived, and especially in what I am living. Death is not frightening. In a sense, death does not lie in front of me but just behind me.[55] When I was born I overcame death, and the more I live the more I am distancing myself from my (deadly) non-being before the time I was.[56] I can put my life at stake at any moment. It is not that I am playing with death. I am playing with life.[57] I do not need to capitalize on life. Life is not just the continuation of a passive state of being, not just the inertia of a static situation, but a constant struggle, the active participation in the cycles of nature in which life does not die.[58] The bearer of life passes it on and thus *he* does not pass away, because the bearer is just what he carries. A quenched torch is not a torch; the torch is the living flame.

It is significant to reflect on the fact that in monetary terms, while prehistorical Man uses roughly 90 percent of his income for food, the citizen of the so-called (historically) developed countries spends only 10 percent. But food for "natural" Man is not just swallowing proteins or preserving health. Food is dynamic communion with the entire universe, food is sharing in the cosmic metabolism, it is the symbol of life, the intercourse with all that there is, the greatest bond among humans and equally the greatest sign of fellowship.[59] The vital needs of historical Man lie elsewhere.[60]

If Joy is the main value for nonhistorical consciousness and Joy is real in the present, Hope is the basic value of historical Man and Hope is tested in controlling and dominating the future. You cannot enjoy three square meals a day, but you can very well produce and accumulate unlimited foodstuffs for use as future political and military weapons.

But prehistorical Man is haunted by the past. If he forgets it, then only those who can remember have the knowledge and the power. Tradition is powerful because it transmits the past. The forgotten past becomes what later is called the mythical past. Cult makes it present. Liturgical time is not historical: the past irrupts into the present: the present transforms the future. Since at least the Upper Paleolithic period (around 35,000 B.C.) we find the same custom of burial, which is Man's first known way of reacting to time.[61]

We have been saying "prehistorical Man" as a concession to historical consciousness and in order to stress the kairological dynamism as seen from a historical perspective. For this reason, I have called this first moment "nonhistorical consciousness." If, in fact, a certain type of this consciousness is represented by the so-called prehistoric peoples, another type of the same consciousness has existed in far more recent cultures, like most of the major traditions of Asia. The time–awareness is certainly nonhistorical and it would be improper to suggest that these cultures must now catch the last wagon of historical consciousness, as we shall have opportunity to explain. One of the most powerful factors in the world today is the Myth of History, which renders plausible the effort to spread the Western–originated technological worldview around the world under the pretense of its universality.[62]

But before we proceed further, we have still to characterize the other two moments.

III. HISTORICAL CONSCIOUSNESS

In the second moment, the previous kairological phase is not discarded but it is progressively superseded, or at least counterbalanced.[63] This new period, the period of the Script, also marks the passage from *agri*culture to *civi*lization, i.e., from the village to the city. The village, like the fields and nature, does not have that specific time which we today call human. City time is not so much cosmic as it is historical. It does not move so much with the sun as with the clock.[64]

Historical time is not just human time, although historical Man tends to identify them. It is this identification which gives birth to the Myth of History. Historical time is that particular (human) time–consciousness which believes in the autonomy of the "human" race vis-à-vis the time of terrestrial and superterrestrial entities. And this historical time, called "human" time, is mainly understood as the thrust toward the future—in which the fullness of existence or definitive welfare, be this of the individual, the tribe, the nation or all humankind, will be achieved. This human time implies the conviction that we are in bondage, not yet completed, and for that reason we must struggle against Nature, against Fate, against the Earth or Matter. It is a struggle for Freedom against anything supposedly antagonistic to Man. Our destiny is (in) the Future.

While nonhistorical time–consciousness may find man's fullness in the very temporal moment, historical time is indefinite and needs to be "rescued" (redeemed)[65] in eternity or in a qualitatively different future if Man is to be saved from the sisyphean despair of never achieving anything or reaching any goal. Historical Man, unlike prehistorical Man who stands in greater or lesser harmony with Nature, believes himself to be in dialectical opposition to Nature. The civilized Man is the non-natural (cultural) human being.[66] Both the belief in a future eternity and the belief in an eternal future belong to the same need that historical consciousness feels, namely, to transcend temporality.

Here transcendence is the main category. You have to transcend time.[67] You have always to go beyond and ahead.[68] You have to travel and conquer space. You have to set sail for the Indies, even if you get no further than the Americas. You have to fly to the moon and explore beyond the limits of your power, even if it explodes in your hands (or over the heads of the Japanese), even if genetic manipulation will make you a puppet in your brave new world. You cannot stop.

Immanence, on the other hand, is the main category of nonhistorical consciousness. We should draw attention here to the double meaning of the word immanence.[69] It is significant that from the perspective of historical consciousness the concept of immanence has been interpreted as a sort of negative transcendence; otherwise immanence, for an historical mentality, would be synonymous with identity.[70] But immanence can also be understood in a nonhistorical way, and in this case it means neither negative transcendence nor identity. That the Divine Spirit, to give an example, is immanent in us does not mean that God dwells in us in such an interior way that we are transcendent, so to speak, with respect to the Spirit—who would then be demoted to the status of an inner guest. Nor does it mean that there is a sort of monistic identity between the "two" (God and the soul). It means (although the word "meaning" may not be appropriate here) that we may be able to distinguish—but not separate—them, that they are neither one nor two, without for that matter saying that the distinction is only an epistemological one. The mystics, in the historical world, indeed have such an experience. But one does not need to be a mystic at all in order to have such a "vision" of things.

Nonhistorical consciousness is geared to immanence, we said, as historical Man is to transcendence. For this nonhistorical consciousness to be happy, to realize its own full humanity, there is no need to go out and conquer the moon or another space (or in a male dominated society) another woman, just for the sake of having another experience. Instead one tries to discover what one is and what one has, one prefers to be spectator rather than actor, one will perhaps kill one's woman before just trying another one—or if she has gone off with another male.[71]

Village life has, in this sense, no "historical" future.[72] Even today, if you want to have a career, you go to the city.[73] Village time has its seasons, its past and future; the year is its unit; but the presiding value is the present as conditioned by the past. And for the present, for the encounter with a friend, the celebration of a feast, a marriage, or for going to war, village Man may easily endanger and even sell his entire future.[74] The fight against the dowry system in India, for instance, is bound to fail (like Western-style family planning) if the problem is not tackled at this deep anthropological level.[75] It may be worth noting that the alleged incapacity, in the eyes of so many "social workers," of so-called undeveloped peoples to accept and adopt the "benefits" of modernity may simply be (human) nature's reaction to external onslaughts. The modernized technocrats call it the passive resistance of the primitive mentality, impervious to change and suspicious of technical improvements—"for their own benefit," of course. This instinctive resistance of the "natives" is very often their defense mechanism for self-identity and survival. At any rate, the greatest rupture introduced by modern technology in nontechnological cultures is precisely the breakdown of their autochthonous rhythms by the introduction of a foreign time–consciousness.[76]

It may spare us long pages of description to recall a familiar story of the Biblical tradition, and to become aware of the biased sympathy of that tradition for its hero, considering his dubious, lying character.[77] Esau was a prehistorical Man; Jacob had historical consciousness. The former was unconcerned about the future and found in the exquisite taste of a potful of lentils the fulfillment of the present, and thus of life.[78] He cared nothing for his historical destiny. Instead, he believed in the symbolism of eating.[79] The latter was concerned with what has been the dominant feature of Semitic civilization: the coming of the Kingdom—variously called promised land, nation, church, heaven, paradise, justice, liberation or whatever. Jacob understood the meaning of his grandfather's move out of the city of Ur and into the future. He was eager to be the heir. Esau did not care about history, about historical vocation, historical destiny, about a task to be performed by the power of his or God's will outside and beyond the actual reach of his person. His sense of transcendence was not temporal. The Indian peasant who sells off his entire future for the dowry of his daughter, or the African family which consumes all its reserves for the great annual celebration is on the side of Esau. Christ irritated the children of Jacob when he told them to let the day take care of itself and not to worry about the morrow.[80] Historical Man has to think about the future and has to live towards it. Prehistorical man has no historical role to play or function to perform. His life is lived in the present, although often haunted by the past. He sings and lives like "la cigale," while historical Man works and hoards treasures like "la fourmi" of La Fontaine's fable. Again, any bank official in the villages of India or elsewhere will tell you how these "primitive" people have no idea of savings and wring his hands over how difficult it is to "educate" them into the paneconomic ideology. Now they are told that to look after their old age they will need not grandchildren but money—inflation notwithstanding. Historical time is under the spell of the future and the guidance of reason. What Esau did was not reasonable, nor was what Christ preached.

People and peoples are set whirling into motion; their movement accelerates not because they want to overcome space or be victorious over it, as nomadic tribes or prehistorical Man might do, but because they want to conquer *time,* as well as to demonstrate their excellence and superiority over others (a superhuman role). Wars are waged to make the victors great and their children powerful. Man works under the mirage of an historical future to be achieved: a great empire to be built, a better future to be conquered, an education for the children, to make ends meet, etc.[81] The entire Modern economic system is based on *credit,* i.e., the mortgage of the future.[82]

This sense of purposefulness and ambition are the essence of Modern education. Modern Science means the ability to foresee the future, so that you may control where the ball is going to fall, or predict when the eclipse is going to occur, or insure your longevity. We need only substitute atoms, bombs, chromosomes and epidemics for balls; and upheavals, inflations, crystallizations, amalgams and synthetic products for eclipses; and we have spanned 6,000 years of human "science:" the knowledge and control of those parameters expressible in terms of space and time.[83] It is important to bear in mind that what we call Science, understood as the attempt to control empirical causality, began as Magic. The paramount question here is to know *how* things will happen in space and time—because then you can *control* them.[84] Space and time become the paradigms of reality. Something is real for us when we can locate it on the grid of spatio–temporal Cartesian coordinates. From here we immediately deduce that something is real when it is a fact, and, when the "fact" belongs to the past, it has to be an historical fact. Jesus is considered to be real if he is an historical figure—whereas Kṛṣṇa, for the nonhistorical Hindu mentality, would lose his reality if he were to be described as only an historical personality.

The growth of historical consciousness did not reach its maturity until the birth of Modern Western Science, although its origins are much more ancient, as any History of Civilization or Science will tell us.[85] Both forms of consciousness are intermingled. One does not have to accept Kant's conception of time and space as forms a priori to our sensibility to realize that cultures and civilizations have not always experienced the two of them, first of all, as intrinsically connected, and then not always in the same manner.

The world of historical Man, his environment (*circumstantia, Umwelt*) is the *anthropocosmos,* the human world, the universe of Man. Historical Man is not inserted in the evolution of the cosmos; his destiny has little to do with the fate of the stars, the phases of the moon, the seasons or the rivers.[86] He lives in what he believes to be a superior world, the human one; cold and heat, day and night, rain and drought have been overcome. He is not dependent on the seasons, and as little as possible on the climate. The seasonal feasts of the Catholic Church, to take an example from a relatively traditional institution, have practically disappeared.[87] Nature has been tamed and subjugated. It has been demythicized, there is nothing mysterious about it. Its secrets have been unravelled and its power channelled into megawattage and megatonnage of all sorts. Historical consciousness has overcome the fear of nature. The meaning of life is not to be found in the cosmic cycle but in the human one, in society, which is a human creation. *Justice* is the supreme principle—which does not mean that it has been achieved. Nor has historical consciousness gained all the hearts and minds of our contemporaries. Prehistorical attitudes and reactions are still powerful.

By the same token, the world of historical Man is not the world of the spirits. Angels, apsaras, devils, dwarves, elves, devatās, sirens, goblins, seraphim, bhutas and the like have all been, if not completely done away with, rendered impotent and subservient to human reason. In any event, these ghosts have no history and historical Man's life no longer unfolds on such a stage—despite occasional outbursts of the ghostly, irrational unconscious.[88] The only scene is the historical arena. With the DDT of his reason, Man has allegedly rendered all forces innocuous. If at all, they are energies to be studied by psychoanalysts, psychiatrists, parapsychologists (if need be), physicists and so forth. Historical life is a display of Man's possibilities before his fellow humans. Historical Man stands alone in the world theatre—without Gods or other beings, living or inanimate. If some still accept God, he is transcendent, impassive, perhaps good for another life but certainly not about to meddle in human affairs. God has left the world to the strivings of men.[89]

If the discovery of Script could be said to have been the decisive break between prehistorical and historical consciousness, the corresponding event here—which opens up the post-historical period—is the discovery or invention of the internal self-destructive power of the atom. So powerful is its nature that it has ceased to be what it was purported to be: *aksaram,* indestructible. It has ceased to be *atomos,* indivisible, ultimately simple and, in a certain sense, everlasting. The splitting of the *atomos* has also exploded historical consciousness.[90]

We are not yet fully aware of the anthropological (and not only political and sociological) consequences of that fact. This change is qualitative, not only in weaponry and technology, not only in the nature of war and the mechanism of the economy, but also in the newly emerging self-understanding of Man. When Becquerel less than a century ago (1896) proved that the atom was destructible and thus not immutable, he shook the belief of millennia of civilization: that the world is made of some permanent elements, whether they are called elements, ideas or principles. At any rate, the atom stood for the consistency of things held to be permanent and thus reliable. The atom corresponded to the old idea of substance. If nothing "sub-stands" anything, historical consciousness is at a loss. There is no platform, no beginning from which anything can unfold and upon which can be accumulated being, experiences, energies or whatever. Modern physical science knows better, but old beliefs die hard. At least elementary particles and their interaction with energy seemed immutable. Now this also is put in question.[91] Nothing seems to escape the corrosive passing of time. Or perhaps time itself is a constituent of a more embracing reality?[92]

This change may well represent the end of the Western period of humankind. There is no doubt that the acme of historical consciousness is tied not only to the Judaeo-Christian-Islamic tradition but also to Western dominance of the entire planet, even if the name for such dominance is Science and Technology. The grandeur of the idealistic view of history, of a Schelling calling History "the eternal poem of the divine Reason,"[93] or Hegel's identification of History with Reason,[94] or Marx's equation of History and Science,[95] or even more recent characterizations of Man as history:[96] all this comes to an end.[97]

IV. THE CRISIS OF HISTORY

As long as several historical realms and empires of all sorts were on the planet, Men could go on believing that the cruelties and inconsistencies of one system could be corrected by another, and that, at least theoretically, historical existence was the destiny of the human being. To be sure, many empires supposed they had conquered, dominated or at least influenced the entire human race, but we know that until now not a single historical regime has pervaded the four corners of the world. Nor have we yet come to such a pass, and this gives us some small respite.[98] But Science and Technology are on the brink of penetrating everywhere, and the paneconomic ideology is more and more becoming the only system of "communication." Moreover, the world situation is dominated by the politics and policies and the two so-called superpowers and their respective (more or less reluctant or "nonaligned") satellites. We are fast heading toward one single System, despite the dialectical divergences of the protagonists on the world scene. It is this situation which leads ever more people to wonder whether such an impasse can really be resolved simply by emigrating from a socialist country to a capitalist one, by improving the System, or by transcending history altogether. This is what I must perforce call not *an* historical crisis à la Toynbee, but *the* crisis of History, i.e., the crisis of historical consciousness as the underlying common and prevalent self-understanding of Modern Western Man and his cultural satellites.

Of course it is quite obvious that a numerical majority of the peoples of the Earth do not live within these parameters. Nonetheless, their lives are increasingly affected by the historical power. Let us try to catch a glimpse of the situation.

First of all, we have to distinguish three final stages: the end of History, the end of Time and the end of Man. Before the secular spirit made its inroads into the Western mind the majority of the world believed in the end of Man. Even if there may be a second cosmic cycle this Man, as we know him, comes to an end—and generally by a catastrophe. If in the Hindu and other oriental traditions there are indefinite *kalpas* or cosmic periods, in the Abrahamic traditions there is only one. But the final act is a catastrophe. I am not speaking *directly* about this.[99]

I am also not speaking about the end of Time, but about the end of History. I am precisely disentangling these two issues by questioning the assumption that Man is exclusively an historical being.[100] So I am not addressing myself to the traditional theological question, but presenting an anthropological problem. The Myth of Progress has practically collapsed.[101] The *historical* situation of the world today is nothing less than desperate.[102] There is really no issue of "development" for the famished masses which make up over half the world's population.[103] There is no consolation for the millions who have been mentally and physically handicapped by malnutrition.[104] It is no answer to proclaim that modern technology *can* overcome all these shortcomings when in fact it *cannot* alleviate the present predicament of those who are in the meantime victims of this situation, and it *does not* solve all the problems it could (utopically) resolve. What is worse, people have lost all hope that the lot of their children is somehow going to be better. And their common sense prevails. They are already in the third generation of those "evangelized" by the hope of a technical paradise, and they have reached the end of their tether.[105] This is the situation today: the heavenly Paradise has lost its grip on most people. A life of privation here, a vale of tears now, a bad karma in this life so that I may be rewarded later on with a heavenly Garden, a city of Brahman, a vision of God or a more comfortable rebirth—all these are rapidly receding myths.[106] Election discourses and traditional religious preachings may still stir the masses for an emotional moment, but the human race is becoming more and more immune to such societal viruses. The goods have to be delivered now, and not when God and the (i.e., my) Party is going to win.

But there is not only despair among the poor. There is equally disenchantment among the rich. The poor of the world still retain a certain prehistorical religiosity which gives them something to hold on to. Those who live in scientific and technological comfort have discarded the Gods and now find that their practical Supreme Value shows signs of radical impotence.[107] The rich would justify their comforts by persuading themselves that "in due time" the masses would also enjoy them. Now we can no longer believe it. It is ingrained in the System that the rich get richer and the poor poorer.[108] But no solution is at hand and we have lost innocence.[109] Post-industrial society is becoming increasingly conscious that the trend of the present world cannot be stopped. Standstill would amount to chaos.[110] Armaments proliferate to maddening proportions—and have to, or else the present economic system would collapse tomorrow.[111] The paneconomic society is bound to explode sooner or later.[112] If you quantify everything and put a price-tag on every human value, the *humanum* vanishes and gives way to the *monetale.* Every "human" good becomes subservient to its monetary value. Some privileged people may prosper, but happiness will elude them. But there is still more to it: today we realize that *the people* will not prosper, only some individuals, groups, classes or nations.[113] An economy based on mere profit is bound to burst the day you have no more markets to make the operation profitable, because all the "others" are living at a much lower standard than you are. Commerce means exchange, not profit. But who in the Modern world would be satisfied with just exchanging goods? The moment that human values become monetizable, you need an incentive to run commerce.[114] Profit, not the joy of discovery or the curiosity of novelty or pride in your courage, becomes strictly necessary.[115] To this day, among the tribes of Nagaland in Northeastern India, rice is not *sold,* i.e., one does not speculate with the elementary needs of life; they do not have a market value but a human value.[116] Fundamental human needs should be out of the economic bounds. We do not eat human flesh, not because it is not good or nutritious, but because it is human. Yet today, even if we do not kill our fellows to eat their flesh, we let them sell their rice and starve in consequence.[117]

We had best consider for a moment some examples. The entire world economy today, and with it the world of politics as well, is geared to the historical future under the name of growth and the power of credit.[118] And here the trouble begins. The Modern world is beginning to surmise that there may well be limits to growth.[119] In the world of the Spirit growth has no limits because the Spirit as such has no limits: growth does not mean *more* but *better.* So here we have another theological idea gone berserk; a theological thought (the infinity of God) becomes a cosmological belief (the infinity of Matter). But in terms of quantifiable matter, better has to mean more: more accumulation of more finite entities into a finite recipient. Growth of this sort can quickly become cancerous. No wonder that cancer is the modern epidemic! Nowadays, faced incontrovertibly with the finite material resources of the planet, the urge to grow has been vitiated. But the momentum of growth seems inexorable. It cannot stop itself unless a qualitative change takes place, and the hope for such a change is the congruous Marxian worldview. Otherwise a catastrophe or a dictatorship is welcomed, if only to contain the runaway growth—because those who can have more at the price of others having less will not divest themselves of their advantages out of sheer moral principles. Of course a mere cataclysm would only lead people to repeat the vicious circle all over again. Most of the words of warning we hear today were already articulated after the First World War, but no heed was paid to them. He who rides the tiger cannot dismount it. And this seems to be the predicament of our Modern world.[120]

Let us keep to the example of the Modern economy. Capitalism is geared to profit and, by an internal logic, to the maximum of profit. The passage from the *optimum* to the *maximum* is linked with the passage from the present to the future.[121] Credit means mortgaging the future in the hope that work will redeem it in due time. Here again the model is one of infinite time.[122] We are impelled to live toward the future. Disenchantment sets in when we can no longer work for the problematic welfare of our great grandchildren, because even for those we can still see around us the System is ineffective. Historical consciousness finds itself in an impasse. Historical consciousness seeks its fulfillment in the future but the internal logic of an economy of profit and growth, unlike a lifestyle of contentment and self-sufficiency, inherently obliges one to mortgage the future. You do not grow from the inside, like a living organism, but by enrichment and accumulation from the outside. Such a situation is literally a *mort-gage:* a pledge to die once the markets become saturated and the victims, called clients, reach the limits of their endurance.[123] Historical Man claims to control and forge his destiny. Yet the present human predicament seems utterly to have escaped his control.[124] And it is this problem of control that produces the current crisis of historical consciousness.[125]

Totally different is the economic vision of most traditional cultures, which are so often labelled "primitive." They function under

three assumptions which are at loggerheads with the Modern paneconomic ideology:
1. Regional welfare versus a global economy.
2. Regional self-sufficiency versus global profit.
3. Limits to the value and restrictions on the field of the economy, versus extrapolating it as a universal value in a universal field.

It is clear that by embracing the entire planet, Modern communications have undermined assumptions (1) and (2). But it is also clear that the change (often called progress) is proving to be worse than the previous stage.[126] Self-sufficiency is destroyed in favor of profit the moment you accept the principle of interest.[127] And profit is only for the successful ones. Success here means to be *better off* than your neighbor. The medieval western theologians who argued against usury as an antinatural device, i.e., against the idea that money generates money,[128] were not so wrong after all when they pointed out not only the antievangelical spirit of the practice but also the principle of exploitation of Man by Man inherent in the Modern economy.[129] It is the very system that calls for human exploitation.[130] It is abuse as a System.[131] But we have reached the limit: global profit is self-contradictory. The British, the Banias, the Medicos can only expand as long as there are underprivileged masses.[132] Now we reach three limits: that of humanity, of its patience and of the Earth itself. There are not many new markets left; there is not much endurance left in the people, now conscious of being exploited by the System; and energy consumption can no longer be expanded without devastating ecological convulsions. The internal economic dialectic is deceptively simple. In a closed system, the profit of one party entails the loss of another party. The only way to widen the system is to multiply money. This is inflation. It gives momentary relief to those who do not need it for subsistence, but thrusts deeper into the pit those who are at the bottom.

Modern economy is the natural counterpart of an egalitarian society. Once all hierarchical distinctions are levelled down—no castes, no guilds, no aristocracies—the only differentiating factor becomes money, which is one's way of distinguishing oneself from others.

The contemporary political panorama is no longer that of a children's quarrel, and the social disintegration cannot be brought under control. Competitive society is bound for self-destruction. If success means reaching the top, the moment others are alerted so that they too can reach it, they will try to destroy you, and one another after that. Past and present examples are only too blatant. The situation is not that of a battle between the good guys and the bad guys, the white and the black, Americans and Russians, believers and unbelievers and so on. The struggle is with the System to which the human world seems to be inextricably bound: the technological and paneconomic ideology.[133]

Again, it is not convincing to say that technology *in itself* is not bad or that money *as such* is a handy invention; because there is *no itself* and *as such*. Abstractions will not do, just as reason alone will not solve any human problem, because the human situation is not an exclusively rational one. Abstraction is a good scientific method but inapplicable to human questions, because nothing human can be subtracted from Man without changing the very variables of the problem.

My contention is that the contemporary technologico-paneconomic ideology is intrinsically connected both with historical consciousness and with the specific character that consciousness has taken in the Judaeo-Christian-Islamic-Marxist-Western world. The Western roots of Modern Science have been sufficiently studied and this is equally the case with technology, which could only be what it has turned out to be with the collaboration of the present economic System of the West.[134] The entire predominant System today presupposes not only a certain epistemology and anthropology linked with the emerging new cosmology, but ultimately a whole ontology.[135]

Paolo Freire's "conscientization" and most of the movements for achieving political consciousness in Latin America, Africa and Asia represent the painful passage of the pre-historical consciousness of so-called illiterate masses into historical consciousness.[136] In fact they are passing from the pre-scriptural mentality to an historical mentality.[137] The villagers and even more the recent immigrants into the urban slums are being exploited because of their lack of historical consciousness. Modern political and social reforms tend to "conscientize" these people by giving them a sense of history, by inciting them to be actors in history and authors of their own destiny, instead of mere objects of exploitation.[138] They are taught to organize themselves and struggle for their rights. It is when they enter history, however, that they discover the great deception: they have come too late, and cannot be the masters of history.[139]

Let us put it in very crude terms. Many people are afraid of a Third World War and a major atomic catastrophe. (Another example of projecting our fears as well as our joys into the future.) Those who feel such panic are generally the well-to-do denizens of the First and Second Worlds. But for two-thirds of the people of the world, that cataclysm has *already* come.[140] Please ask not only those living in sub-animal conditions (again, much over one-third of humankind); please ask the millions of displaced persons, and take a look at the geopolitical chart of the world (since one can scarcely call it a human map): Gulags, concentration camps, persecution and real wars on every continent. *The Third World War has already come,* and the atomic phase of it will be only the predictable outcome and final act of a drama which is now not only Myrdal's "Asian Drama" but a World Tragedy of massive proportions and devastating implications.[141]

I have elaborated these more sociological aspects of the contemporary world so as to emphasize the urgency of the question, its importance and the existential background for a trans-historical consciousness. This latter is no longer the privilege of an aristocracy but begins to be the common lot of the people and peoples of the Earth in their search for survival amidst the internal and external strains of Modern life.[142]

In sum, the Historical Imperative has failed.[143] All messianisms lose their raison d'être.[144] And yet the two great political superpowers of the day both have in common the messianic idea that they represent and embody the salvation of the world.[145] At this eleventh hour, however, the impasse begins to appear with greater and greater lucidity to more and more people. The symptoms are legion: the possibility of global human self-destruction, the depletion of the Earth and the conquest of Space, the planetary interdependence of humankind and the universal vulnerability to any clever individual or self-seeking group, the increasing fears and indeed the new defense mechanisms for survival—no longer geared to a more powerful technology but to a new thrust toward life, independent of the powers that be. The conviction is equally gaining ground that the present-day economic System can no longer be controlled by external factors, that it is on the contrary this very System which conditions the options and imposes its dominance. Reform is no longer a solution, and Revolution only amounts to turning the same mechanism upside down.

History has become not a dream but a nightmare. Man, said to be an historical being, discovers that he cannot make History. Dictatorships render the people powerless, and democracies have failed not only in the praxis but in the theory. The individual—when there are millions of them—does not really count, any more than a single dollar counts when the transaction is on the order of billions. The individual is only a powerless fraction in a mass. In order to have power, one would need to cease being an average person—since to join with others to form a pressure group requires above-average means, especially when the group has to be of a size which only technology can manage. The majority has become a mass, which as such is ill-equipped to discover any truth.[146] Moreover, when the issues at stake are global questions, issues of survival and not just technicalities, what justification has a country (or its ruling elite) or a group of countries for imposing the burden of its policies on the rest of humankind? The minority can bow to the majority when it comes to driving on the right or the left side of the road, or changing the decimal system, but when you are threatened in your very being, the limits of tolerance have been reached.[147]

And yet the individual is left with the conviction that he can do little to alter the force of circumstances, the inertia of the System or the dynamism of Power. More and more the conviction dawns upon the human spirit that the meaning of life does not lie in the future or in shaping society or transforming Nature but in life itself lived in its present and actual depth. To this recently more visible—although not novel—moment in human consciousness we now turn our attention.

V. TRANSHISTORICAL CONSCIOUSNESS

This third form of consciousness is coming more and more to the fore.[148] The two others are far from having disappeared and, to be sure, this third form has always been in the air in the shape of metaphysical insights and mystical experiences. But today it is gathering momentum, and by virtue of the principles elaborated by the Sociology of Knowledge it is also changing in character.[149]

As both symptoms of the crisis of historical civilization and attempts to find a way out, there are today all over the world movements for Peace, Non-Violence, Return to the Earth, Disarmament, Ecology, World Federation and what have you, right down to Macrobiotics. Most of these point to a trans-historical mood, but they should take heed lest they contribute to prolonging the agony of life in an unjust System by not being radical enough. Without something of a trans-historical dimension, even these movements run the risk of being co-opted into the System. An example would be the "social services" which allow "business as usual" to march on unabated without the bad conscience occasioned by coming face-to-face with its victims, merely because some good souls are taking care of them.[150] We may, and even must, join in the efforts for a better world and a more equitable social order, but we should not deceive ourselves. It is here that the function of the true intellectual and/or contemplative becomes paramount. What we need is a radically different alternative, not just patchwork reform of the abuses of the existing System—in spite of the fact that any practical steps toward this alternative will have to begin with the *status quo* and try to convert it into a *fluxus quo* conducive to a New Heaven and a New Earth, if this much used and abused image is still permissible. In any event, such an alternative demands nothing short of a radical change in consciousness.

Let me suggest at least one of the roots of this radical change. In Western parlance, I would put it that we are witnessing the passage from monotheism to trinity, i.e., from a monotheistic worldview to a trinitarian vision. In Eastern words, it is the overcoming of dualism by advaita, i.e., the transition from a two-story model of the universe to a nondualistic conception of reality. In philosophical language, it boils down to finding the middle path between the Scylla of Dualism and the Charybdis of Monism.[151] In a more contemporary way of speaking, we could say that it amounts to experiencing the sacredness of the secular.[152] I mean by secularity the conviction of the irreducible character of time, i.e., the sense that Being and Time are inextricably connected. Time is experienced as a constitutive dimension of Being; there is no atemporal Being. *Sacred secularity* is an expression meaning that this very secularity is inserted in a reality that is not exhausted by its temporality. Being is temporal, but it is also "more" and "other" than this. Now this "more" is no mere juxtaposition—as if eternity, for instance, would arrive "after" time, or as if a supra-temporal Being were temporal "plus" something else, or merely atemporal. Similarly, this "other" is not another Being which does not share temporality. I would use the word *tempiternity* to express this unity. Employing another neologism[153] I have called *cosmotheandrism* the experience of the equally irreducible character of the divine, the human and the cosmic (freedom, consciousness and matter), so that reality—being one—cannot be reduced to a single principle.[154] This is, in my opinion, the basis for a change which is truly pluralistic.

If we take pluralism not as a political strategy but as a word representing the ultimate structure of reality, we shall have to overcome the assumption of a single human pattern of intelligibility.[155] At this level, all words break down.[156] It may be that there is only one scheme of intelligibility, but we cannot postulate it *a priori*. It may also be that there is a peculiar awareness of dimensions of reality which simply does not fit into the category of intelligibility.[157] We may be aware of Matter or of the Spirit and yet be unable to call them intelligible—not only *de facto,* because *we* cannot (*quoad nos*) know them, but *de iure* (*quoad se*) because *they* do not belong to the order of intelligibility.

The underlying hypothesis of monotheism is that there is a Supreme Mind to which all things are intelligible, so that if *quoad nos* beings are not transparent, *quoad se*—i.e., for God—all reality is intelligible.[158] It would not be fair to criticize this metaphysical hypothesis by underscoring the dangers of manipulation and the abuses it has led to in all sorts of caesaropapisms, totalitarianisms and colonialisms, East and West.[159] The problem is of a deeper nature.[160]

To say that we are beginning to witness the end of history does not have to mean the end of Man. Yet the ordeal is going to have historical proportions, precisely if we are to bring history to an end. In this crucible of the Modern world, only the mystic can survive.[161] All the others are going to disintegrate: they will be unable to resist either the physical strictures or the psychical strains.[162] And this disintegration will include the so-called middle classes which for the moment can eat adequately, and do not try to take a stand on any slippery decision-making platform. The bourgeois, i.e., the inhabitants of the burghs, are today the denizens of the megalopolis: bombarded by noise, haunted by fear, drowned in "information," propagandized into stupefaction; people anonymous to one another, without clean air to breathe or open space for human—and not just animal—intimacy, with no free time at all because time itself is now in bondage.[163] There is no real *scholè,* leisure, and time is no longer free.[164]

The mystic, or at least a certain kind of mystic, has a trans-historical experience. He or she does not situate things along the course of linear time. Theirs is a vision which includes the three times: past, present and future.[165] An example is the difference between the popular belief in the Semitic religions of a "creation" at the beginning of the world, understanding this creation as an event situated in the past, and the interpretation often given by metaphysicians and mystics that "creation" and "conservation" of the universe by God are not two separate acts and that creation is a continuous process.[166] Scholastic theology affirms that the simplicity of God obliges us to say that the very act by which God begets the Son creates the world.[167] The eternal intra-trinitarian process and the temporal extra-trinitarian act ultimately coalesce in their source. In this vision, the fulfillment of my life does not need to depend on the fulfillment of the historical future of my nation, people, race or even humankind. I am somewhat independent of the strictures of historical events. If the end of my life is the destruction of all *karmas* still binding me to the temporal flux, then the meaning of human life no longer lies in the historical fulfillment of a mission but in the realization of the human being.[168]

Prehistorical Man was fearful of Nature, but he managed in his own way to come to terms with Mother Earth or the Earth Goddess. Now Big Brother and his twin, Technology, are frightening historical Man, who tries desperately to cope with them. Prehistorical Man had to take his distance from Nature, so to speak, in order to survive as Man. It is this alienation from Nature that made him Man and differentiated him from the animals—for better or worse. Modern, i.e., historical Man has now to separate himself from *the System* in order to live as Man. It is this salutary severance, this weaning from the System that will differentiate those who succeed in preserving their humanness from the robots, victims of the System: ants, work-addicts, cogs in the megamachine, "bits" identified by number in the ubiquitous computers' memory banks. Withdrawal from the System does not necessarily mean flight into the mountains or mere escape from history. It certainly does mean a pilgrimage to the "high places" of the human spirit and the human Earth, as well as the overcoming of the historical obsession. But it also means keeping one's hands and heart free to help fellow beings on their way to this new conscientization. Perhaps we could call it *Realization.*

Here are some of the traits of this Realization: Nonhistorical consciousness sees life mainly in the interplay between the past and the present; the future has hardly any weight. Historical consciousness is busy discharging the past into the future; the present is just the intersection of the two. Trans-historical consciousness attempts to integrate past and future into the present; past and future are seen as mere abstractions. Not only has the two-story building of prehistorical Man collapsed, but the one-story building of historical Man is also a shambles. The two-story building was the cosmological image of traditional religions: now and here are only the time and place for the struggle to attain the happiness of salvation elsewhere and after.

Here is where we should situate Buddhism, as that wisdom which is based on the experience of the momentariness of our existence, without accumulations from the past or expectations for the future. We have here an example of a nonhistorical but certainly not prehistorical mentality: the Buddhist *kṣaṇavāda* or doctrine of the momentariness of all things (of all *dharmas*). Reality is basically discontinuous.[169] We create time. Time does not sustain us like a mother. It is our child. The only reality is the creative instant. History is woven from the detritus, as it were, of authentic human activity, and of any activity. History may have to do with *karma*.[170] Both are factors impinging on our lives, and we must rid ourselves of them.

Human life is more than just an accretion from the past and a projection into the future. It is both (and together) the *ex* and the *sistence* which constitute our being. This is why only by in-sisting on the ex-sistence are we saved. And this is the experience of contemplatives. They live the present in all its in-tensity and in this tension discover the in-tentionality and in-tegrity of life, the tempiternal, ineffable core which is full in every authentic moment. It is the *Nunc dimittis* of old Simeon realizing that his life had been fulfilled in the vision of the Messiah,[171] or the *hodie* of Christ to the good thief:[172] Paradise is the today, in the *hic et nunc,* but not in their everyday banality or in the externals of death and suffering. That is why, I submit, Christ said to the good thief: "You shall be . . ." The future of the *today* is not tomorrow; it is in trespassing the inauthenticity of the day in order to reach the *to-day* in which paradise abides. The meaning of life is not tomorrow, but today.[173] To be sure, between the two moments there is a chasm, there is an abyss. This abyss is death. One has to have overcome death in one way or another. Only then have we the care-free living of the mystics, the nonaccumulation of riches of the Gospel, the transcending of space and time of the Hindu, the momentariness (*kṣaṇikatva*) of the Buddhist, the Nothingness of the Chinese, and so on.[174]

The novelty of the phenomenon is the increasingly societal aspect of trans-historical consciousness on the contemporary scene.[175] It is no longer some few individuals who attempt to overcome historical consciousness by crossing to the other shore and experiencing the transtemporal, the tempiternal. There are increasing numbers of people in the historical world impelled to this breakthrough in their consciousness out of sheer survival necessity, due to the stifling closeness of the System and the universal strictures of the Modern predicament. It is precisely the instinct for survival that throws many toward the other shore of time and space, because the spatio–temporal framework of this Earth is being polluted and prostituted beyond measure by the mechanical robots of the megamachine, all victims of the technological cancer.

We are assisting at a change in the relationship between the sociological strongholds of these forms of consciousness. Pre-industrial societies tended to be inclined to nonhistorical consciousness—not only in the East, but also in the West.[176] Now post-industrial societies are becoming more and more open to trans-historical consciousness while the "elites" of the pre-industrial societies are trying to change the mode of consciousness of their countrymen in order to introduce the historical consciousness which is a prerequisite for industrialization, or for revolution.[177]

The generalized belief of the nonhistorical mentality, which still penetrates deeply into historical times (we spoke of kairological moments) is this: only a very few reach salvation.[178] Salvation is a privilege.[179] Reality is hierarchical. Just as only one is the king or only a few seeds among millions bear fruit, so the elect are the exceptions among Men. The others are either aborted from this new life or will be given other chances in successive births. Heaven is for the few; the gate is narrow; few are chosen. All this is in the realm of transcendence or the "next" life, even if this is understood mythically.

Historical consciousness transforms this belief in another world into an historical vocation to an historical future.[180] The historical belief in Israel of a certain type of Judaism and in the Perfect Society of a certain type of Marxism could offer us two typical examples, although we could also adduce many a Christian and Muslim belief. Fulfillment is in the future.[181]

The religious crisis of historical humanity sets in when the conviction dawns that this future does not look very bright in either the vertical or the horizontal directions. Another world as a sublimated replica of this one loses credibility, and another world in the near or distant future has, practically speaking, missed its chance to carry any power of conviction. Confronted with this situation, trans-historical consciousness gains ground among the peoples.

But the democratization of Modern consciousness, the leveling down of the hierarchical structure of the universe, destroys the belief that salvation or realization is a privilege. Man wants the fulfillment of life not only here and now for the select few, but for everybody. This means that there is now emerging a new myth that the fullness of life— or more simply, its meaning—has to be attained not only in this world, as the mystics have always stressed, but for everyone. This salvation, understood as human fulfillment, cannot be tied to, or belong to, one race, one culture, or one religion. Modern conscience feels that it has to be universal, within reach of everybody. Yet it is obvious that this is not the case; a substantial proportion of the four billion humans have not even reached the minimum level of the *humanum*. It is this impasse that fosters the emergence of trans-historical consciousness on a societal level, once the great temptation is resisted: the fall into hedonistic indulgence in the merely temporal moment by those who can selfishly afford it. This may be said to be the traditional touchstone of authentic spirituality. Escapism from the people, instant self-gratification, selfish elitism and blindness to the historical predicament of Man would be just the opposite of the trans-historical consciousness I am describing.[182]

Summing up: The background of prehistorical Man is the *theocosmos:* He finds himself in friendship and confrontation with the *numina,* the natural and divine forces. His scenario is the divinized cosmos.[183] He lives mainly turned toward the past. He worships his ancestors.

The horizon of historical Man is *history:* He finds himself in collaboration and struggle with human *society* of the past, present and future. His world is the human world. He lives mainly turned toward the future. He worships the God that shall be.

The emerging myth of trans-historical Man assumes a more or less conscious *theanthropocosmic* vision of the universe: He finds himself, in varying degrees of harmony and tension, within a cosmotheandric *reality* in which all the forces of the universe—from electromagnetic to divine, from angelic to human—are intertwined. He lives mainly in the present. He is very cautious in worshipping. If at all, he would reverence the intersection of past and future, of the divine and the human.

Prehistorical Man has *fate*.[184] He is part and parcel of the universe. Historical Man steers *destiny*.[185] He predestines where he stands. He arranges his own life. Trans-historical Man lives his *lot*.[186] He is involved in the total adventure of reality, by participating in the portion "allotted" to him, or by willingly shaping the part that he is.

The prehistorical mentality does not have to justify Man's existence, to itself or to others. The human being simply lives, like any other living being. Historical consciousness has to justify, i.e., to prove, the value of Man's existence by his *doing,* i.e., by creating or producing his own world with its values. Modern Man is a worker.[187] Trans-historical Man has lost both the prehistorical naiveté and the historical optimism/pessimism. He feels the urge to be what he is supposed to be by occupying his proper place in the universe.[188]

The world of trans-historical Man, his environment, is the cosmotheandric universe. The renewed interest in astrology, for instance, is due not merely to the desire to know what will happen, how a marriage or a business will develop, but to the increasing awareness that personal destiny is linked both with the fate of society and with the adventure of the entire cosmos. As another example, we may cite the renewal of popular religiosity and the proliferation of so many new religious movements expressing people's thirst to connect again not only with the human world but with the universe at large, where humans are not the only conditioning forces. The destiny of Man is not just an historical existence. It is linked with the life of the Earth and with the entire fate of reality, the divine not excluded. God or the Gods are again incarnated and share in the destiny of the whole universe. We are all in the same boat, which is not just this planet Earth but the entire mystery of Life, Consciousness, Existence. *Love* is the supreme principle, the linking force which brings everything together. But we have already hinted at the main reason for the awakening of such consciousness: that life has to make sense even when all the idols—progress, civilization, peace, prosperity, paradise—fail. To make virtue of such a necessity does not make the virtue any less real, once it is truly achieved.[189]

We could formulate the same fundamental intuition from a personalistic perspective. All Men want to reach salvation. I take this statement to be a qualified tautology. All Men want to acquire the fullness of what they believe they are called to be. All Men want to be happy— another translation of the same tautology. But it is a qualified tautology because it implies that all Men want to reach the meaning of their lives and it opens the door to different understandings of that meaning by calling it Salvation and allowing a variety of notions as to what this salvation may be. Now we could describe three fundamentally different interpretations or experiences of this Salvation, according to the predominant degree of consciousness. In most religions we find the three types, although with differing emphases. For the purposes of our discourse, we may call one *nirvāṇa,* the other *sotería* and *mokṣa* the third.[190]

Nirvāṇa, as the name indicates, would suggest here a "blowing out," an exhaustion of the burning material, an escape from the strictures of the prison of space and time and thus of matter. I save myself by allowing *samsāra,* this world, to fall quietly away, even if to do so I must put up with it for the time being and do my duty. My salvation consists in the realization that I was already immortal, except that I was enmeshed in this trap of matter. The examples here would run from Plato and the Gnostics to Mahāvira and the Vedāntins. They cross religious boundaries, because the source could be said to be the personal experience that my being is ultimately pure consciousness (or simply a soul) and that this consciousness or soul has nothing to do with my body or, ultimately, with matter.

Sotería, as the name indicates, implies a being whole and healthy, protected and well. It entails a belief in the possibility of transforming the structures of space and time into something that will provide Man with the very fullness of his being. One is saved when one reaches that condition of a New Heaven and a New Earth where the deep and authentic nature of everything will shine forth in its true state and make manifest the universal harmony which is now veiled, distorted or rotten—owing to whatever disorder: personal, cosmic or divine. Immortality is not something which belongs to one's nature but something that belongs to the redeemed structures of the transformed universe. It has to be not only conquered but recreated, as it were. It is a new creation. The examples here would run from Paul and the Christian Fathers to Abhinavagupta and the Tantrikas. They cross religious boundaries because the source could be said to be the personal experience that my being is a mixture of spirit and matter that has not yet arrived at its complete fusion, and that this integration is ultimately the very meaning of reality.

Now it is clear that if the ideal of salvation is *nirvāṇa,* the historical development of the world is a very secondary process, relevant only insofar as it touches one's self directly, making one suffer or giving one enough to eat and live on, so that one may pursue the real goal of one's life.[191] Contrariwise, if the ideal of salvation is *sotería,* the historical development of the world impinges directly on my own realization and that of all my fellow beings. To be engaged in the historical process of transforming humankind is the means for salvation.[192]

Traditional religions have been inclined to interpret salvation as *nirvāṇa* in a more or less radical or qualified manner. So traditional Christians would consider this world not as an obstacle, perhaps, but as a means to attain the other, the real one. Modern movements such as Marxism and Humanism have been inclined to interpret salvation as *sotería* in a more or less radical or qualified manner. The great crisis of our times is that *nirvāṇa* has ceased to be credible to a great part of the world, mainly to that part of humankind which has been touched by the ideology of Modern Science. And, at the same time, *sotería* has equally lost its credibility for a great part of humankind presently facing the no-exit of the present paneconomic ideology. Is there any way out of the dilemma? Is there a trans-historical human experience above and beyond the nonhistorical *nirvāṇa* and the historical *sotería*? If *nirvāṇa* is fundamentally transcendent, and *sotēría* immanent, *mokṣa* could be the code for this rather nondualistic interpretation of the problem. The peoples of the world thirst for this integral liberation, not only from the chains of an unjust social order but equally from the limitations of a confining, selfish ego.

In sum, trans-historical consciousness is not worried about the future because time is not experienced as linear or as an accumulation and enrichment of moments past, but as the symbol of something which does not exist without Man but cannot be identified with him either. It is neither the City of God nor the City of Man that trans-historical Man is about to build. He or she would rather concentrate on building or bringing to completion the microcosm that is Man, both individually and collectively: mirroring and transforming the macrocosm altogether.

Separated, any one of these three modes of consciousness is insufficient to bear the burden of being human. Not unlike the androgynous character of Man (in spite of the differentiation between male and female), these three modes are all intertwined in human life, although kairologically distributed.

My essay here has been to render plausible the thesis that the exclusive dominance of the Myth of History on the one hand, and historical consciousness on the other, are both coming to an end. Man is embarking upon a new venture, about which we know only that we shall act the more freely the more we allow the internal dynamism of our deepest being to express itself, without projecting beforehand what we are to do and to be. We are creatively participating in the very existence of the cosmotheandric reality.

NOTES

1. Cf., for example, Lewis Mumford, *The Conduct of Life,* New York (Harcourt Brace Jovanovich) 1951, 1970, especially chapter VIII, "The Drama of Renewal." Mumford includes many such critiques.

2. The author is fully aware of the difficulty and danger of hurried syntheses and generalized overviews; but for many decades he has been concentrating on the problem of a "Visión de sintesis de universo" (*Arbor* 1 [1944]) and would like to offer these late reflections as an homage on the centenary of his birth to Pierre Teilhard de Chardin, who was not afraid of breaking all anthropomorphic scales and applying to Man the parameters of the evolution of the Cosmos.

3. "Il est difficile de saisir l'intelligibilité d'un mythe à partir de l'autre, mais on doit admettre qu'une bonne partie du monde aujourd'hui est aterrée à

la pensée de la possibilité d'un cataclysme à l'échelle planétaire, tandis que toute une autre partie de l'humanité n'est pas trop touchée par le déclin historique de la race humaine." R. Panikkar, "L'eau et la mort," M. M. Olivetti (ed.), *Philosophie et religion face à la mort,* Paris (Aubier) 1981, p. 500.

4. Cf. R. Panikkar, *"Colligite Fragmenta: For An Integration of Reality",* in F. A. Eigo (ed.) *From Alienation to At-Oneness* (Proceedings of the Theology Institute of Villanova University), Villanova, Penn. (Villanova University Press) 1977, pp. 35 sq., where I have developed these three moments from a more general perspective. Both essays belong together and complement one another. In the present study, I concentrate on the human consciousness of the temporal reality.

5. After years of using this word I find that Romano Guardini had the following scheme: "Das Dasein verwirklicht sich in der Zeit," and, in consequence, "heissen die drei Teile der christlichen Lehre von der Daseinzeit die Archelogie, Eschatologie und Kairologie." He describes the latter as the doctrine of the moment: "wie die laufende Zeit gegenwärtig und damit das Dasein in jeweils unwiederbringlicher Einmaligkeit dem Menschen anvertraut wird; abermals das Dasein des Einzelnen und der auf ihn hin bestehenden Welt." *Die letzten Dinge,* Würzburg (Werkbind-Verlag) 1940, Introduction (without page number). There is an English translation by Ch. E. Forsythe and G. B. Branham, *The Last Things,* Notre Dame, Ind. (University of Notre Dame Press), 1965. First edition: Pantheon Books, 1954.

6. The word *period* comes from the Greek (*peri*) (around) and (*hodos*) (way and also manner). Cf. 'episode' (*epi-eis-hodos*), 'method' (*meta-hodos*), etc.

7. The *kairos* would emphasize the nonlinear and especially nonhomogenous aspect of time, over against the *chronos,* notwithstanding the fact that *kairos* and *chronos* were often used indiscriminately in Greek. *Secular* would underscore the experience of the *saeculum* as the temporal life span of both the world and the human being.

8. I had hesitated between *para*-historical and *meta*-historical, but the current use of the first prefix and the different utilization of the second one in different contexts has decided me to use the prefix *trans-,* though I must insist on its secondary meaning—i.e., not so much in the sense of trans-cendence, of going *beyond,* as of trans-parency, passing through.

9. For the complexity of the human experience of time, cf. J. T. Fraser (ed.) *The Voices of Time,* New York (Braziller) 1966, and J. T. Fraser, *Of Time, Passion and Knowledge,* New York (Braziller) 1975, and again J. T. Fraser, *et al.* (ed.) *The Study of Time.III,* New York (Springer) 1978, all works of the International Society for the Study of Time. I have completed a bibliography on time of more than 1,500 entries. Cf. my forthcoming book on *Temporalia.*

10. I say "generally" because nonhistorical consciousness is prevalent in many of the Asian and African cultures of "today"—using this last word in a chronocentric historical way.

11. We shall not discuss here the evolution of this threefold consciousness or, for that matter, how far prehistorical Man can be said also to possess historical and trans-historical consciousness.

12. I should state at the outset that Man with a capital "M" refers to the entire human being—*anthropos*—previous to the differentiation of the sexes.

13. It would require an elaborated anthropology to properly explicate these parentheses.

14. Cf. Bartṛhari's memorable beginning:

This brahman without beginning and end,
primordial word, imperishable, which appears
as objects and from which
the living world comes . . .

(*anādinidhanam brahma śabdatadttvaṃ yad akṣaram/'rthabhävena prakriyā jagato yataḥ*)

15. Cf. the fifteenth century European play *Everyman,* possibly of Buddhist origin according to the author of a new version, Frederick Frank, *Every One,* Garden City, NY (Doubleday) 1978.

16. "Global perspective," "total awareness," "universal outlook" and similar expressions are useful and well-intentioned signs of the will to overcome dangerous provincialisms, but they are impossible ideals for any single human being. This universalism could in its turn become a new source of totalitarian or colonialistic attitudes: "We have the global vision, we know better and impose our ideas upon you—for your own benefit, of course!"

17. "Thinking" here stands for the overall human intellectual activity, related to consciousness and including, of course, the (conscious) will and thus love.

18. Cf. Aristotle, *Metaphysics* IX, 8 (1050 a23–b2); etc.

19. Paradoxically, we could say that if this *praxis* reveals Reason for Hegel, it should be shaped by Reason for Marx. Cf. also the texts of Kant, Gentz, Rehberg in *Über Theorie und Praxis,* with an Introduction by D. Henrich, Frankfurt a.M. (Suhrkamp) 1967, for the discussion surrounding Kant's polemical paper.

20. The meaning of the root *"Fid",* from which "historia" comes, is to see, to know. Cf. "eidos," idea; "histor," the erudite, he who knows and witnesses, the judge. "historikos-e-on" means exact, precise (scientific) and "historeo" to enquire, observe, examine.

21. Hegel distinguishes "History" as *historia rerum gestarum,* the subjective aspect, and as *res gestae,* the objective aspect, in *Vorlesungen über die Philosophie der Geschichte, Werke,* edited by H. Glockner, XI, 97.

22. Cf. Hegel's central and masterful *Die Vernunft in der Geschichte,* and the well-known quotation at the end of his *Philosophy of History:* ". . . for the history of the world is nothing but the development of the idea of freedom."

Translated by J. Sibree in *Great Books of the Western World* (R. M. Hutchins, ed.), *Hegel*, Chicago, etc. (Encyclopaedia Britannica) 1952, p. 369.

23. Cf. W. Dilthey's description of his enterprise of a "Critique of Historical Reason:" "d.h. des Vermögens der Menschen, sich selber und die von ihm geschaffene Gesellschaft und Geschichte zu erkennen," *Gesammelte Schriften*, I, 116 (apud Scholtz, art. *Geschichte*, in J. Ritter (ed.) *Historischen Wörterbuch der Philosophie*, Darmstad (Wissenschaftliche Buchsgesellschaft) 1974, vol. III, 382). Dilthey sees clearly, "dass der, welcher Geschichte erforscht, derselbe ist der die Geschichte macht."—*Schriften*, V II, 278 (*ibid.*).

24. Cf. M. Heidegger's first description: "Geschichte ist das in der Zeit sich begebende spezifische Geschehen des existierenden Daseins", *Sein und Zeit*, Tübingen (Niemeyer), 12th ed., 1972, p. 379. And also "Das Dasein hat faktisch je seine 'Geschichte' und kann dergleichen haben, weil das Sein dieses Seienden durch Geschichtlichkeit konstituiert wird" p. 382. Obviously the entire work should be consulted, especially the last two chapters of the book. We cannot now enter into the complete problematic.

25. Cf. Schelling's saying that the only content of philosophy is history (*Werke* - ed. K. F. A. Schelling, I 382 sq.) Apud Ritter, *op. cit.*, III, 363. An idea which the Romantics will also reiterate.

26. Cf. R. Panikkar, "Words and Terms," *Archivo di Filosofia* (ed. M. M. Olivetti) Roma 1980, 117–133.

27. "Homeomorphism is not the same thing as an analogy; it represents a peculiar functional equivalence discovered through a topological transformation." It is "a kind of existential functional analogy," R. Panikkar, *The Intrareligious Dialogue*, New York (Paulist Press) 1978, p. xxii.

28. Cf. G. Steiner, *After Babel—Aspects of Language and Translation*, London (Oxford University Press) 1975, and the abundant bibliography.

29. Cf. R. Panikkar, "The Supreme Experience," Chapter X of *Myth, Faith and Hermeneutics*, New York (Paulist Press) 1979.

30. Cf., for details and justifications, the study by Alfons Rosenberg, *Durchbruch zur Zukunft, Der Mensch im Wassermannzeitalter*, Bietigheim/Würt. (Turm Verlag), with no date, although the second edition is of 1971.

31. For the beginnings of the Aquarian Age, cf. the controversy surrounding Marilyn Ferguson's book *The Aquarian Conspiracy*, Los Angeles (J. P. Tarcher) 1980, in *Forum* XI, 1 (1980), pp. 27–46; although my perspective here is probably more radical.

32. Interestingly enough, the literal reckoning of the age of the world according to the Bible would be precisely 6,000 years.

33. Cf. an example of such experience in my study "El presente tempiterno: Una apostilla a la historia de la salvación y a la teología de la liberación" in *Teología y mundo contemporaneo* (Homenaje a K. Rahner) ed. by A. Vargas-Machuca, Madrid (Christianidad) 1975, 133–175, where an alternative is sug-

gested to the dilemma of non-Western cultures either perishing or accepting historicity.

34. The epochal daring of Teilhard de Chardin consists in projecting straightaway the miniscule *homo sapiens* into the galactic destiny of the universe. The present study may well provide a missing link between the cosmological macrolevel and the anthropological microlevel.

35. We cannot really pursue the argument further here. Cf., as a single reference because it is not very well-known, F. Ebner's *Das Wort und die geistigen Realitäten* and *Zum Problem der Sprache und der Worter,* both reprinted in *Schriften I,* München (Kösel) 1963.

36. I am not contesting the legitimacy of Teilhard's approach. I am perhaps offering the vital connection between history and cosmology. But I refrain from discussing the problem of evolution.

37. "Nur die gesamte Menschheitsgeschichte vermag die Massstäbe für den Sinn des gegenwärtigen Geschehens zu geben", wrote Karl Jaspers in 1949 just after the Second World War, *Vom Ursprung und Ziel der Geschichte,* Frankfurt a.M. (Fischer) 1956, p. 11. One generation later, I dare to add that the application of this scale leads to the conclusion that we are on the brink of the mutation already suggested. This is what Jaspers seems to indicate at the end of his book: "Die Auffassung der Geschichte im Ganzen führt über die Geschichte hinaus." p. 262.

38. One thing seems certain. Our solar system has already lived half its life span. The planet Earth is a mortal macro-organism. Our boundaries are not only spatial, but temporal as well. From this perspective, we are all prisoners. But this is not our question here.

39. To lump Genghis Khan and the Mongol invasion of Europe together with the French Revolution and the Chinese Cultural Revolution, to toss the Punic Wars into the same sack with the last two World Wars—because all are but microscopic moments of a cosmic evolution towards a noosphere—may help us to discern a general direction of the universe, but it tends to blur the equally necessary distinction between the exploits of a Hannibal and those of a Hitler.

40. How often a Roman Catholic is confronted with outsiders who tell him or her: "But you cannot speak this way as a Catholic!", for they have learned in the Baltimore Catechism what Catholics should believe and consider the Catholic tradition fixed once and for all. Similarly, "philosophers" charge "scientists" with having to stick to paradigms that men of science have long ago discarded. Or, for that matter, "scientists" tend to imagine that philosophers just do not have the tools to understand them. For the relations between science and philosophy, cf. my book *Ontonomía de la Ciencia,* Madrid (Gredos) 1961.

41. Cf. also my study "The Myth of Pluralism—The Tower of Babel," in *Cross Currents* XXIX, 2 (Summer 1979), pp. 197–230.

42. It would be interesting to relate together H. Nakamura's *Ways of*

Thinking of Eastern Peoples, Honolulu (East–West Center) 1964, and M. Heidegger, *Was heisst Denken?*, Tübingen (Niemeyer) 1954.

43. I have inserted this paragraph after the discussion of this paper at the Georgetown University Celebration of the Centennial Symposium in honor of Teilhard de Chardin, in order to circumvent some possible misunderstandings.

44. Plato, *Phaedrus,* 274–275. It is worthwhile enough to reproduce the entire passage:

Socrates: But there remains the question of propriety and impropriety in writing, that is to say the conditions which make it proper or improper. Isn't that so?

Phaedrus: Yes.

Socrates: Now do you know how we may best please God, in practice and theory, in this matter of words?

Phaedrus: No indeed. Do you?

Socrates: I can tell you the tradition that has come down from our forefathers, but they alone know the truth of it. However, if we could discover that for ourselves, should we still be concerned with the fancies of mankind?

Phaedrus: What a ridiculous question! But tell me the tradition you speak of.

Socrates: Very well. The story is that in the region of Naucratis in Egypt there dwelt one of the old gods of the country, the god to whom the bird called Ibis is sacred, his own name being Theuth. He it was that invented number and calculation, geometry and astronomy, not to speak of draughts and dice, and above all writing. Now the king of the whole country at that time was Thamus, who dwelt in the great city of Upper Egypt which the Greeks call Egyptian Thebes, while Thamus they call Ammon. To him came Theuth, and revealed his arts, saying that they ought to be passed on to the Egyptians in general. Thamus asked what was the use of them all, and when Theuth explained, he condemned what he thought the bad points and praised what he thought the good. On each art, we are told, Thamus had plenty of views both for and against; it would take too long to give them in detail. But when it came to writing Theuth said: "Here, O king, is a branch of learning that will make the people of Egypt wiser and improve their memories; my discovery provides a recipe for memory and

wisdom." But the king answered and said, "O man full of arts, to one
it is given to create the things of art, and to another to judge what
measure of harm and of profit they have for those that shall employ
them. And so it is that you, by reason of your tender regard for the
writing that is your offspring, have declared the very opposite of its
true effect. If men learn this, it will implant forgetfulness in their
souls; they will cease to exercise memory because they rely on that
which is written, calling things to remembrance no longer from within
themselves, but by means of external marks. What you have discovered is a recipe not for memory, but for reminder. And it is no true
wisdom that you offer your disciples, but only its semblance, for by
telling them of many things without teaching them you will make
them seem to know much, while for the most part they know nothing,
and as men filled, not with wisdom, but with the conceit of wisdom,
they will be a burden to their fellows."
Translated by R. Hackforth, *Plato, The Collected Dialogues,* Hamilton
and Cairns (ed.), Princeton (Bollingen/Pantheon) 1961, p. 520.

45. Cf. the classical study by M. Nilsson, *Primitive Time–Reckoning* (A
Study in the Origins and first Development of the Art of Counting Time among
the Primitive and early Culture Peoples), Lund (C. W. K. Gleerup) 1920 for
examples, data and arguments.

46. Cf. *Ṛg Veda,* X, 135, 1; although, significantly, it is a hymn describing
the ancestors in the realm of Yama.

47. Cf. the famous pre-Socratic sentence attributed by Aristotle to Thales
(*De Anima,* I, 5 (411 a7–8), and already reported by Plato (*Laws,* X (899 b)):
"Of all the planets, of the moon, of years and months and all seasons, what other story shall we have to tell than just this same, that since soul, or souls, and
those souls good with perfect goodness, have proved to be the causes of all,
these souls we hold to be gods, whether they direct the universe by inhabiting
bodies, like animated beings, or whatever the manner of their action? Will any
man who shares this belief bear to hear it said that all things are not 'full of
gods'?"
Translated by A. E. Taylor, *Plato, The Collected Dialogues, op.cit.,* p. 1455. Cf.
also Aristotle's *Metaphysics* I, 3 (938 b 20–27) and Augustine's *De Civitate Dei*
VII, 6 (MPL 41,199) on Varro's dictum of the world's elements "full of souls."

48. An important aspect which would throw light on a characterization of
this first mode of consciousness would be a study on the human attitudes toward sex. Cf. E. Aguilar, *Vers una sexologia de la religió* (pro manuscripto),
1981, where the scattered data on paleolithic Man are gathered with a view to
determining both our present deepest instincts and the basic experience of prehistorical Man.

49. *Non numero horas nisi serenas* (I do not reckon but the sunny hours), says an ancient sundial.

50. Cf. the significant passage of Hegel: "Was wir eigentlich unter Afrika verstehen, das is das Geschichtlose und Unaufegeschlossene, das noch ganz in natürlichen Geiste befangen ist, und das hier bloss an der Schwelle der Weltgeschichte vorgeführt werden musste." *Die Vernunft in der Geschichte*, ed. by J. Hoffmeister in Philosophische Bibliothek, 171a (5th ed., 1955), p. 234. Apud Ritter (ed.), *Historisches Wörterbuch der Philosophie, op. cit.*, Vol. III, 1974, *sub voce Geschichtslosigkeit*, where J. Burckhardt's opinion is also given: The barbarism of the "barbarian" is precisely this "Geschichtlosigkeit" (lack of any sense of history).

51. The bibliography is already becoming immense. Cf. the recent studies:

F. Gillies, "The Bantu Concept of Time," *Religion*, X (Spring 1980), 16–30.

J. Murungi, "Toward an African Conception of Time," IPU, XX, 4 (December 1980), 407–416. On Ameru time–reckoning.

A. Kagame, "The Empirical Apperception of Time and the Conception of History in Bantu Thought," in UNESCO, *Cultures and Time*, Paris (UNESCO) 1976, pp. 89–116.

52. Hegel had already seen that "das Historische" begins where "die Zeit des Heroentums," i.e., the age of the culture hero, ends. *Werke* (ed. H. Glockner) XIV, 256 sq . (Apud Ritter, *op.cit.*)

53. It is significant that the most obvious meaning of the Second Coming as described in the New Testament and the Resurrection of the Flesh as maintained by the dogma of the Church, namely that it all happens in a nonhistorical context, has been almost overlooked in Christian exegesis. To put it quickly: individual Final Judgment and humanity's Last Judgment, for the individual, coalesce. The Second Coming arrives at the death of each human being. The Resurrection is with our identical body of flesh and bones, i.e., now. Cf. R. Panikkar, "La Eucaristía y la Resurrección de la Carne" (1952), reprinted in my book *Humanismo y Cruz*, Madrid (Rialp) 1963, 335–352.

54. Matthew, VI, 34.

55. Cf. R. Panikkar, "The Time of Death: The Death of Time. An Indian Reflection," in *Meletê Thanatou/ La réflexion sur la mort* (Ecole Libre de Philosophie "Plethon." 2ᵉ Symposium International de Philosophie) Athènes, 1977, pp. 102–121.

56. Cf. for instance the typical Buddhist mentality where Long-ch'en Rabjam-pa said in the XIV century: "The suffering of birth is more fearsome than that of death." *Dharmacatur-ratnamâla*, 1 (transl. by A. Berzin, *The Four-Themed Precious Garland*, Dharamsala (Library of Tibetan Works and Archives) 1979, p. 19.

57. Many of the hunters' customs which have prevailed until our times

among the military and which books of history record as gladiators, soldier's bravery, duels, etc., could be adduced as examples. The most recent one could be gathered from the—on the other hand frightening remarks—of the President of the United States of America, Senators and Congressional Representatives, when two Libyan planes were shot down over the coast of Libya on August 19, 1981. Just an exercise to prove that "America has the muscle to back up its words." (R. Reagan, as reported in the *Santa Barbara News-Press*, August 21, 1981, p. 1). You look at the present and the past, but not at the future. The difference, however, with modern weapons in a volatile world, cannot be over-estimated.

58. Cf. *Chāndogya Upanisad* VI, 11, 3.

59. Cf. for example the Vedic texts on food, which although already of a late period still reflect this mentality, apud R. Panikkar, *The Vedic Experience*, Los Angeles/Berkeley (University of California Press) 1977, pp. 224–237.

60. "You North Americans"—some business executive was complaining—"eat in between the working hours; we South Americans just work between the hours of eating!"

61. Cf. for data and elaboration S. G. F. Brandon, *History, Time and Deity*, Manchester (University Press) New York (Barnes & Noble) 1965. Brandon's overall thesis "is that religion has stemmed from man's consciousness of Time, and that his reaction to Time has found a variety of expressions including the deification of Time." "The Deification of Time" in *Studium Generale* 23 (1970) 485–497.

62. From this viewpoint, both the so-called First and Second Worlds, the Liberal Capitalist and the Socialist Capitalist ideologies are just two variations on the same historical myth. For an understanding of the Second World as "those (few) countries which, at somewhat different times but far ahead of the rest, were able to take advantages of the techniques while escaping the mental, political or economic control of the First World," cf. D. V. Coutinho, *Cross Currents*, XVIII (Fall 1968). Yet our present-day situation shows that what might have been a difference at the beginning has been eroded if not destroyed by the very power of Technology (First World).

63. It should be clear that I do not subscribe to the simplistic evolutionary theory still prevalent today in many History and History of Religions books which regards "prehistoric Man" as an undifferentiated and unevolved primitive whom "we" have now left completely behind us. The process is much more complex, and we find today not only in the so-infuriatingly-called Underdeveloped Countries, but also (fortunately) in each of us, strong traces of primordial Man. Cf. my *Colligite Fragmenta, op. cit.*

64. "Abstract time became the new medium of existence," says L. Mumford in his chapter "The Monastery and the Clock," where he defends the thesis that "the application of quantitative methods of thought to the study of nature had its first manifestation in the regular measurement of time." With the clock,

"Eternity ceased gradually to serve as the measure and focus of human actions." *Technics and Civilization,* New York (Harcourt, Brace and World) 1963, pp. 12–18 (first edition, 1934).

65. Cf. Eph. V, 16.

66. Cf. the popular distinctions between Nature/Culture, World/Person, Nature/Grace (Supernature), Man/Animals, Spirit(Mind)/Matter, etc.

67. "Ut ergo tu sis, transcende tempus" ("so that you be, transcend time"), says the first European, the African Augustine, *In Joan.* tr. 38, n. 10.

68. *Plus ultra* (further beyond) was the motto of Charles V of Europe.

69. Cf. R. Panikkar, *The Trinity and the Religious Experience of Man,* New York (Orbis) 1973, pp. 29 sq.; 33 sq.; 59 sq.

70. Cf. R. Panikkar, *Le mystère du culte dans l'hindouisme et le christianisme,* Paris (Cerf) 1970, pp. 29–41. This is the reason why the historical West has so often considered as pantheism and monism the trend toward immanence of many Eastern worldviews.

71. The example of the male–female relationship should be taken "cum grano salis" and understood in this context without extrapolation. What is suggested here is that sexuality can also be envisaged under the attitude of transcendence and that of immanence. Androgyny and the interiorization of the *śakti* could be examples of the latter.

72. Cf., for instance, J. S. Mbiti, "The African Conception of Time," *Africa* VIII (1967), and other writings of the same author, who maintains that African traditions have "virtually no concept of the future;" although his view is contested by F. Gillies, *art. cit.*

73. As the saying goes, "In the village, young man, you have no future. You'd better take a job in the city."

74. "Are you going to live in debt for the rest of your life? Don't you realize that this momentary celebration of just a few days will represent a mortgage on your future?"—says the westernized "well-to-do" Man to whom the villager has gone to ask for a loan for the marriage of his daughter. The villager understands so little of this discourse that he is hardly capable of replying: "But don't you understand that life is made of such moments? Don't you realize that life is only worth living if we celebrate it by giving it away? Are you not capable of eating time, assimilating it and making it your own, so that you don't have to slip on it as if it were something external to you?"

75. And at this level, of course, the problem presents itself in a different light.

76. This begins to be felt even by modern Westerners in their own lives. The proliferation of technological means for overcoming the limitations of space and time is now reverting and producing precisely the contrary effect. Cf., as an example, J. P. Dupuy, "L'encombrement de l'espace et celui du temps," *Esprit* 10 (October 1980), pp. 68–80. Also especially noteworthy is Ivan Illich's essay "Energy and Equity," London (Calder & Boyars) 1974, recently reprinted

in Illich, *Toward a History of Needs,* New York (Bantam) 1980, pp. 131–172.

77. Cf. Gen. XVII, 1 et seq. Would it be fair to say that historical cities, kingdoms and countries have mostly been founded on violence, blood and deceit? History only leaves a place for the victors. *Vae victis!*

78. It is remarkable how Esau has been downgraded as a glutton eager only to fill a biological need—as if Brahman were not food and the Eucharist an eating, as if Communion with Nature were to the shame of "civilized" Man, as if, again, it is only the Future that counts. The basic distinction emphasized by J. Maritain and which—through O. Lacombe, L. Gaudet, R. C. Zaehner and others—has often been blurred in the History of Religions, between immanent nature-mysticism (natural) and transcendent encounter with the living God (supernatural), may also have the same origin in this historical interpretation of reality, which is then superimposed on nonhistorical worldviews.

79. Cf. by way of example, the Vedic texts on Food in R. Panikkar, *The Vedic Experience, op. cit.,* II, 10–11, pp. 224–237: Food is Brahman! Cf. also G. Deleury, *Le modèle indou,* Paris (Hachette) 1978, the chapter on "Les manières de table," pp. 21–40.

80. Cf. Luke VI, 34, etc.

81. Cf. R. Panikkar, "The Mirage of the Future," *Teilhard Review,* Vo. VIII, Nr. 2, London (June, 1973), pp. 42–45.

82. If time, this linear time, were to stop the whole system would collapse. The "most powerful nation in the world" has the highest budget deficit.

83. Cf. I. Barbour, *Issues in Science and Religion,* New York (Harper & Row) 1966.

84. Cf. Nietzsche's saying in *Thus Spake Zarathustra:* "Wherever I found the living, there I found the will to power," as quoted by R. May, *Power and Violence,* New York (W. W. Norton) 1972, p. 19, trying to show that "power is essential for all living things." (19)

85. Cf. the monumental work of P. Duhem, *Le système du monde,* Paris (A. Hermann) 1913–1917.

86. "Neque enim propter stellas homo, sed stellae propter hominem factae sunt," says Gregory the Great, reflecting the "superiority complex" of the emerging Western Christian consciousness. This attitude is comprehensible as a reaction against the tyranny of the "Stoicheia tou Kosmou", the elements of the world, which characterizes the first Christian centuries of European civilization. Cf. R. Panikkar, *Humanismo y Cruz,* Madrid (Rialp) 1963, pp. 123 sq.

87. Quatember days are forgotten; the night of St. John the Baptist remains popular only in some corners of Southern Europe; the cosmological meaning of Christmas and the Epiphany has almost faded away; the rogation triduum before Ascension has been practically abolished; the feasts of the Guardian Angels and of the three great Archangels have been artificially heaped together. Processions for rain, blessings for a good harvest and for do-

mestic animals have remained as folklore remnants in a few "undeveloped" countrysides.

88. More than 50 percent of all hospital beds in the United States are in psychiatric wards.

89. Cf. Eccles. III, 11.

90. This idea of the importance of the splitting of the atom has often been expressed, but most of the time in connection with the first explosion of an atomic weapon on human "targets:" "This atomic bomb is the Second Coming in wrath," said Winston Churchill the day after the explosion. "If I were asked to name the most important date in the *history* of the human race, I would answer without hesitation, August 6, 1945." (Arthur Koestler) "The explosion of the first atomic bomb has become a *para-historical* phenomenon. It is not a memory, it is a perpetual experience, outside *history*. . . . It has no relation to time. It belongs to motionless eternity." (Pedro Arrupe) Emphasis mine and quotations from J. Garrison, *The Plutonium Culture*, New York (Continuum) 1981.

91. Cf. S. Weinberg, "The Decay of the Proton," *Scientific American* (June, 1981), pp. 64–75. The popularized subtitle says: "The proton is known to have a lifetime at least 10^{20} times the age of the universe, but theory indicates that it may not live forever. If it is not immortal, all ordinary matter will ultimately disintegrate."

92. This is in fact the hypothesis of this paper.

93. ". . . nichts, das heiliger wäre als die Geschichte, dieser grosse Spiegel des Weltgeistes, dieses ewige Gedicht des göttlichen Verstandes," *Werke, op. cit.*, V, 289, 306, 309 (apud G. Scholtz' entry *Geschichte* in Ritter's *Wörterbuch*, III, 364.)

94. "Ich will über den vorläufigen Begriff der Philosophie der Weltgeschichte"—so begins Hegel's lecture on *Die Vernunft in der Geschichte*—"zunächst dies bemerken, dass, wie ich gesagt habe, man in erster Linie der Philosophie den Vorwurf macht, das sie mit Gendanken an die Geschichte gehe und diese nach Gedanken betrachte. Der einzige Gedanke, den sie mitbringt, ist aber der einfache Gedanke der Vernunft, dass die Vernunft die Welt beherrscht, dass es also auch in der Weltgeschichte vernünftig zugegangen ist." Some pages later, he says ". . . ihr Individuum (of history) ist der Weltgeist," and further on: "Das eine ist das Geschichtliche, dass der Grieche Anaxagoras zuerst gesagt habe, dass der Nus, der Verstand überhaubt oder die Vernunft, die Welt regiere . . ."

95. "Wir kennen nur eine einzige Wissenschaft, die Wissenschaft der Geschichte," K. Marx - F. Engels, *Werke*, Ostberlin 1956–1968, Vol. III, 18 (apud Ritter, *Wörterbuch*, op. cit., III, p. 374). Marx says something more than that all science is historical: "Die Geschichte ist unser Eins und Alles" (*ibid*).

96. Cf. Heidegger's *Sein und Zeit, op. cit., passim.*

97. Cf. G. Scholtz' excellent article, *Geschichte,* in Ritter's *Wörterbuch,* for useful information and references.

98. I am saying that not only are the Brazilian and African jungles the "lungs" of the Earth, but that the so-called underdeveloped peoples are all that prevents the System from exploding. Once these peoples are "developed," there will be no exit.

99. This is the strictly theological problem which in the Christian tradition is called the *Parousia* or *Second Coming.* Historians of Religion call it the Millennium, and modern theological thinking distinguishes between the History of Salvation and Human History.

100. It is significant that J. Pieper's *Über das Ende der Zeit* speaks about the end of History. Cf. the English translation, *The End of Time,* New York (Pantheon Books) 1954.

101. Vladimir Solovyev wrote in his last book *Three Conversations* in 1900: "I am of the opinion that progress, that is noticeably accelerated progress, is always a symptom of the end." And thus Alfred Weber, after the Second World War: "The outcome of history up to now is that mankind is returning to the dread of the world and existence that is felt by primitive peoples." "Der *vierte,* Mensch oder der Zusammenbruch der geschichtlichen Kultur," *Die Wandlung* (1948), p. 283. Apud J. Pieper, *op. cit.,* pp. 73 and 75.

102. Typical in this respect is the conclusion of William I. Thompson in his widely-read book of some years ago, *At the Edge of History,* New York (Harper & Row) 1971: "Western Civilization is drawing to a close in an age of apocalyptic turmoil. . . . Birth and death are ultimately confusing; to make sense of them we will have to make our peace with myth.

". . . At the edge of history, history itself can no longer help us, and only myth remains equal to reality. . . . And now we sleep in the brief interval between the lightning and the thunder." p. 163.

103. Cf., by way of example, Susan George, *How the Other Half Dies. The Real Reasons for World Hunger,* London (Penguin Books) 1976.

104. The figures are staggering and irreversible. All we can do is try to prevent the situation from worsening. And this is only a theoretical hope, as the experience of the last 30 years sufficiently demonstrates.

105. Food, that gift of the Gods which, according to the *Bhagavad Gītā,* makes a thief of anyone who enjoys it alone without giving anything in return (III, 12), has become a weapon, a military weapon in the hands of the so-called world powers (cf. S. George, *How the Other Half Dies, op. cit.*). The USA alone, i.e., 6 percent of the world's population, consumes 34 percent and controls over 60 percent of the world's energy (some years ago the figure was 40 percent). Cf. S. Turquie, "Efficacité et limites de l'arme céréalière," in *Le Monde Diplomatique,* Nr. 314 (March, 1980), as a concrete example of speculation regarding US policy against the USSR after the invasion of Afghanistan.

106. "Sic transeamus per bona temporalia, ut non amittamus aeterna"

(May we pass through the good things of the temporal world so as not to lose those of the eternal one), Collect of the Latin Liturgy, IIIrd Sunday after Pentecost, is an excellent prayer provided it is not interpreted as an evasion of earthly responsibilities, postponing the heavenly reward to some later "time" or "other" world. Many examples from other traditions could also be given.

107. The literature is already bewildering. Cf., for instance, the recent study by D. Yankelovich, "New Rules in American Life," *Psychology Today* (April, 1981), pp. 35 sq., which although limited to the United States of North America serves as an indicator of the trend of technological societies.

108. Cf. the many penetrating analyses of Denis Goulet on so-called Development, e.g. *The Cruel Choice,* New York (Atheneum) 1971; *A New Moral Order,* Maryknoll NY (Orbis) 1974.

109. If the world were to use the amount of paper that the United States consumes in two years, no tree would be left on the planet. If the peoples of the Earth were to consume units of non-renewable energy at the rate the United States is consuming them, energy exhaustion of the world would come during our generation.

110. Cf., nevertheless, the efforts at changing economies by gearing them into other fields as reported in *The UNESCO Courier—The Arms Race* (April, 1979).

111. Approximately 60 percent of the worldwide economy of the historically and economically "developed" countries is geared directly or indirectly to armaments and so-called "defense." If such markets were to disappear, their economies would collapse, and—since theirs is a way of life based on economic values—their entire civilization would also collapse. Cf. the recent UNESCO Bulletins dedicated to armaments: *The UNESCO Courier—The Arms Race* (April, 1979), and *A Farewell to Arms* (September, 1980).

112. Modern science fiction literature is proliferating. Novels about the end of the world abound. Cf. Gore Vidal's *Kalki* and Morris West's *The Clowns of God,* just as examples.

113. The studies on neo-colonialism, as the examples of Brazil and India show, are most revealing. Because of the size of these two countries, the experiment can still go on, but the price paid in lack of freedom and surfeit of suffering is also well-known. The "prosperity" of such a country is due to the 5 percent of the population who are in contact with foreign markets and can take advantage—i.e., exploit the fact—of cheap domestic labor. This 5 percent benefits by a factor of thousands of per cent. 15 percent of the people share, in varying proportions, the fringe benefits from the "welfare" of the first minority, and 80 percent of the people live in worse conditions than before the "economic boom" and "industrial progress."

114. The shift in meaning of the word "economy" is significant. From "oikos," house and "nomos," law, order; i.e., the order of the house, the household, the administration of Man's housing (*vivienda* in classical Spanish is still

both house and life-style, way of living), it has come to mean the monetary aspect of all human transactions.

115. The art of bargaining and the human aspect of "shopping" in the so-called underdeveloped countries, in contrast to the stiff, joyless and callous reaction of "developed" individuals buying in these "primitive" shops which do not have "fixed" prices, is a quite ordinary example. The objectification—and thus the dehumanization—of human relations begins. Commerce has lost any relation to human intercourse. Still, human nature seems reluctant to admit such a prostitution. Employees in the supermarkets are quite familiar with the gossip and intimate chatter of their clientele, despite "self-service" and credit cards.

116. At harvest time every family receives all the rice necessary for the season and keeps it in great baskets in the first portico of the house. There are private and communal paddy fields. Only now has the "real estate" business begun to get a foothold. And, incidentally, as of 1980 there have hardly ever been any cases of psychotic illnesses.

117. Cf. the evidence produced by S. George, *op. cit.*, and the documentation cited below from *Le Monde Diplomatique*.

118. "Le monnaie de crédit sert ainsi dans le système capitaliste à projeter dans le futur une production accrue grâce a l'utilisation immédiate d'un volume augmenté de force de travail.", G. Kleinschmidt, "Revenir à l'etalon-or?", *Le Monde Diplomatique*, May, 1980. Or again: "Dès lors, en érigeant la recherche de la richesse pour elle-même en finalité du système, le capitalisme devra substituer une normalisation monetaire nouvelle à celle héritée des économies précapitalistes." *ibidem*.

119. Cf., as a single example, the well-known study by The Club of Rome, *The Limits to Growth*, Donnella H. Meadows, *et al.*, New York (Universe Books) 1972.

120. Cryptically, in a slightly different sense, but also prophetically, M. Heidegger writes: "Die Geschichte geht, wo sie echt ist, nieht zugrunde, indem sie nur aufhört und ver-endet wie das Tier, Geschichte geht nur geschichtlich zugrunde." *Einführung in die Metaphysik*, Tübingen (Niemeyer) 1966, p. 144.

121. As an example of the intrinsic dynamism of the paneconomic ideology, both capitalist and socialist, cf. the by now well-studied problem of contemporary hunger. Cf. the series of articles in *Le Monde Diplomatique*, May, 1980, showing how "Par une perversion de la science et de la technologie, les méthodes de production sont portées à un degree of sophistication que seules justifient les lois de la plus-value et du profit. L'énorme concentration des capitaux et autre moyens élimine le paysan, et sa sagesse millénaire, au profit d'exploitations plus "rentable" économiquement." (p. 13).

122. An analysis of the budgets of individuals, societies and, especially, of states, indicates that living with increasing deficits can lead either to a *sanatio in radice* (bankruptcy) or to an upheavel of the creditors, once they are powerful

enough. One cannot go on indefinitely with a negative budget.

123. The bibliography today is immense. Cf. as a single example the multi-voiced dialogue in A. Birou & P. M. Henry, *Towards a Redefinition of Development* (English edition by J. P. Schlegel (ed.)) Oxford/New York (Pergamon Press) 1977.

124. "Geschichtsbewusstsein ist Symptom der Endzeit," says Erwin Reisner, quoted by E. M. Ciorcan, *Écartèlement,* Paris (Gallimard) 1979, p. 17, who adds: "C'est toujours par détraquement que l'on épie l'avenir." (18); and again: ". . . rien de plus aisé que de dénoncer l'histoire; rien en revanche de plus ardu que de s'en arracher quand c'est d'elle qu'on emerge et qu'elle ne se laisse pas oublier." (18/19) "La fin de l'histoire est inscrite dans ces commencements,—l'histoire, l'homme en proie au temps, portant les stigmates qui définissent à la fois le temps et l'homme." (39)

125. "De même que les théologiens parlent à juste titre de notre époque comme d'une époque post-chrétienne, de même on parlera un jour de l'heure et du malheur de vivre en pleine post-histoire. . . . Le temps historique est un temps si tendu qu'on voit mal comment il pourra ne pas éclater." *ibid.* Or again: "L'homme fait l'histoire; à son tour l'histoire le défait." (42)

126. Cf. Ivan D. Illich, *Tools for Conviviality,* New York (Harper & Row) 1973, as well as Illich's many other incisive critiques of "development."

127. Cf. the four articles of Thomas Aquinas, *Summa Theologiae,* II-II, q. 78: *De peccato usurae* where he keeps to the doctrine of the Church, traditional since the first Councils, and yet already makes the obligatory distinctions for a new financial order.

128. The dictum comes from Aristotle's *Politics* I, 3, 23.

129. Cf., e.g., the article *Usury* in the *Encyclopedia of Religion and Ethics,* J. Hastings (ed.), Edinburgh (T. T. Clark) 1921 (latest impression 1971).

130. Islamic theology said much the same. In some Islamic countries today the banks do not lend money at interest, but share as partners in the investments and gains of their clients.

131. For the situation of foreign workers in 1979 in a democratic and "civilized" country like France, cf. J. Benoît, *Comme esclaves,* Paris (Alain Moreau) 1980. The so-called immigrants in France represent 11 percent of the wage-earning population; yet their proportion of wounded or dead is between 22 percent and 50 percent, etc.

132. For how a highly advanced country with no problems of overpopulation, scarcity of land or economic resources, treats its original inhabitants, cf. S. Hargous, *Les indiens de Canada,* Paris (Ramsay) 1980, and also issue Nr. 62 of the Québécois *Journal Monchanin,* XII, 1 (Jan.–March 1979): *Political Self-Determination of Native Peoples.*

133. The world today includes roughly 200 million people living in concentration camps called slums, *favelas,* ghettos, *bidonvilles* and the like. By the year 2000 most probably some billion or more people will be living in the sub-

human conditions of the "inner cities" or outer slums of the "great cities" of the world. Cf. B. Granotier, *La planète des Bidonvilles,* Paris (Seuil) 1980.

134. As one fully elaborated example, cf. the extensive analysis, references and bibliography of Lewis Mumford's two volume magnum opus, *Technics and Civilization: The Myth of the Machine,* New York (Harcourt, Brace & World) 1967, and *The Pentagon of Power,* New York (Harcourt, Brace & World) 1970. A thoroughgoing critique of the megamachine of Western technological culture.

135. Cf. R. Panikkar, "Die Kulturgeschichtlichen Grenzen der Rationalität: Neun Sūtras über die Ratio," to appear in the Proceedings of the *XVI World Congress of Philosophy,* Düsseldorf, 1978.

136. We should carefully distinguish between the Theology of Liberation in Latin America and other movements for liberation on other continents. Yet all seem to have in common "awareness-building" and the assimilation of historical categories.

137. Cf. the contemporary political posters contesting United States involvement in Latin America which say: "TOMAR LA HISTORIA EN NUESTRAS PROPIAS MANOS"—from a mural of the Casa de los Chicanos at the University of California, Santa Barbara. May 1, 1981.

138. "La conscientisation n'est pas la simple prise de conscience. La libération permaente des hommes ou leur humanisation ne s'opère pas à l'intérieur de leur conscience mais dans l'*histoire* qu'ils doivent constamment faire et refaire," say D. von der Weid and G. Poitevin (*Inde. Les parias de l'espoir,* Paris (Ed. d'Harmattan) 1978, p. 112) with reference to Paolo Friere. Emphasis added.

139. This would be my warning to all movements of "conscientization" in countries on the way to (Western) development. Each culture is a whole. Adoption of short-term advantages is a Trojan horse which brings with it the inevitable destruction of traditional structures. On the other hand, isolation is no answer either, nor are most traditions capable of responding on their own to the needs of contemporary Man.

140. During the Year of the Child (1979), a study by the pediatricians of Kerala reported that 60 percent of the children of that State are likely to grow dull-brained due to protein deficiency. But India in 1978 earned 230 crores of Rupies ($2,300,000,000) in foreign exchange by exporting fish and fish products (and Kerala is a fish-consuming population!). The Indian Army in 1979 rejected more than 50 percent of the candidates between the ages of 17 to 21 on medical grounds, and only 15 to 20 percent were found fit. While the diet of those in the United States and Europe includes 35 percent of protein-rich foodstuffs, the African diet includes only 23 percent, Latin America 20 percent and India 10 percent (and in India, 60 percent of the diet is cereals, over against 9 percent in the United States). (Report by C. J. Samuel in *The Indian Express.*)

141. From the Second World War to 1980, there have been over 130 wars

fought on this "peaceful" Earth. From 1500 BC until 1860 there had been at least (for these have been registered) 8,000 peace treaties, of which the majority contain a clause alluding to permanent, not to say eternal, peace . . .
Cf. Bouthoul, *Huit mille traités de Paix,* Paris, 1948, p. 11. Apud. A. Corradini, "The Development of Disarmament Education as a Distinct Field of Study," *Bulletin of Peace Proposals,* Oslo (International Peace Research Institute) March, 1980, p. 220.

142. Here I would also situate the renaissance of interest in monasticism and the contemplative life among people in the post-industrial regions of the world. Cf., for example, Norman O. Brown citing Jakob Boehme: "To rise from history to mystery is to experience the resurrection of the body here now, as an eternal reality; to experience the *parousia,* the presence in the present, which is the spirit; to experience the reincarnation of the incarnation, the second coming; which is his coming in us.

> Our life is as a fire dampened, or as a fire shut up in stone. Dear children, it must blaze, and not remain smouldering, smothered. Historical faith is moldy matter—*der historische Glaube ist ein Moder*—it must be set on fire: the soul must break out of the reasoning of this world into the life of Christ, into Christ's flesh and blood; then it receives the fuel which makes it blaze. There must be seriousness; history reaches not Christ's flesh and blood. *Es muss Ernst sein, denn die Historie erreichet nicht Christi Fleisch und Blut.*
> Boehme, *De Incarnatione Verbi,* II, vii, 1. From Brown, *Love's Body,* New York (Vintage) 1966, p. 214.

143. We need only consider the historical folly of the world situation in terms of the dialectic between the superpowers and the lethal armaments proliferating on the planet.

144. This is the great challenge to the Abrahamic religions—traditional or secular, in the form of Empire, Church, Democracy, Science or Technology.

145. Cf. E. Jahn, "The Tactical and Peace-Political Concept of Détente," in *Bulletin of Peace Proposals,* XII, 1 (1981), 33–43, where it is shown that none of the 'superpowers' have abandoned their belief that peace and justice on Earth can only be brought about if their respective ideologies triumph—by war, or by détente.

146. Cf. J. Ortega y Gasset, *La rebelión de las masas, Obras Completas,* Madrid (Revista de Occidente) Vol. 4, 1966, pp. 113–312, or the English translation, *The Revolt of the Masses,* New York (Mentor Books) 1950.

147. Cf. R. Panikkar, "Tolerance, Ideology and Myth," Chapter II of *Myth, Faith and Hermeneutics, op. cit.*

148. Trans-historical consciousness pierces *through* history to its transtemporal core. The exceptional use of "post-historical" in this paper should be em-

phatically distinguished from the "post-historic man" of Roderick Seidenberg's classic study of the same name, which dissects the new barbarism of contemporary institutions and processes that have (pre)fabricated a lethal collective automaton out of the Image of God; Seidenberg, *Post-Historic Man*, Chapel Hill, N.C., 1950. Cf. also L. Mumford's powerful essay "Post-Historic Man," based on Seidenberg's analysis, which appears as Chapter 34 in Mumford, *Interpretations and Forecasts, 1922–1972*, New York (Harcourt Brace Jovanovich) 1973, pp. 376–387.

149. Here is where I see the existential and practical character of this study.

150. The proof of the present untenable situation is that such "works of mercy" have become tragic: you are a scoundrel if you don't perform them, and a traitor if you do. Again, another pointer toward the trans-historical.

151. Cf. my many studies elaborating and applying this assumption, e.g., "Rtatattva: Preface to a Hindu–Christian Theology," in *Jeevadhara*, Nr. 49, Jan.–Feb. 1979, pp. 6–63; and *The Trinity and the Religious Experience of Man*, New York/London (Orbis/Darton, Longman & Todd) 1973.

152. Cf. my book *Culto y secularization*, Madrid (Marova) 1979, especially pp. 58–61 and 90–100. Cf. also H. Fingarette, *Confucius—The Secular as Sacred*, New York (Harper & Row) 1972.

153. "Il n'y a que les termes nouveaux qui fassent peine et qui réveillent l'attention," says Malebranche, *Traité de morale*, part 1, chap. 6, par. 8.

154. Cf. R. Panikkar, *Colligite Fragmenta*, op. cit., passim.

155. Cf. R. Panikkar, "The Myth of Pluralism—The Tower of Babel," in *Cross Currents*, Vol. XXIX, Nr. 2, Summer 1979.

156. Cf. the Upanisadic dictum: "Whence the words recoil, together with the mind, unable to reach it—who knows that bliss of Brahman has no fear." *Taittiriya Upanisad*, II, 4, 1, (cf. also II, 9, 1).

157. In the wake of the Greek philosophers, the Latin Scholastics distinguished between the knowledge of an existence and that of an essence. On this basis, moreover, Descartes and Leibniz elaborated the entire problematic surrounding the Ontological Argument.

158. Cf. the Thomistic principles: "Deus enim cognoscendo se, cognoscit omnem creaturam.", *Sum. Theol.* I, q.34, a.3, and J. Pieper's answer to J. P. Sartre that existence is not prior to essence because there is an Existence identical to its Essence (God). We could equally adduce Spinoza or Hegel regarding the ultimate intelligibility of Being.

159. Cf., e.g., F. Heer, *Europäische Geistesgeschichte*, Stuttgart (Kohlhammer) 1953.

160. Cf. S. Breton, *Unicité et Monothéisme*, Paris (Cerf) 1981. On totally different lines, cf. David C. Miller, *The New Polytheism. Rebirth of the Gods and Goddesses*, New York (Harper & Row) 1974.

161. This was the cryptic leitmotif of my collection of essays of over 30 years ago, published as *Humanismo y Cruz,* Madrid (Rialp) 1963.

162. The statistics on mental illness are revealing, even without speculating about increases in violence, suicides, assassinations, crime-rates, etc.

163. Cf. E. Castelli, *Il tempo esaurito* Padova (Cedam) 1968, and also *Il simbolismo de tempo,* E. Castelli (ed.), Roma (Istituto di Studi Filosofici) 1973.

164. The very shift in the meaning of the words tells some of the story. To *negotiate,* in English, means to manage, to convert into money. The Latin *negotium* is rightly translated as "business": to be busy, i.e., to have *nec-otium* (no leisure). And here *otium* certainly means peace, calmness, tranquillity. Cf. "affair," from the Latin *ad facere,* to do, be done: ado (trouble, fuss). Cf. equally the etymologies of the German *Geschäft* ("was man zu schaffen hat," what one has to do, produce, create) and *Handeln,* commerce (to handle, i.e. to make with the *hands:* arts and crafts). Even more revealing is the etymology of *work* in the Latin languages (trabajo, travail, etc.) from *tri-palium,* an instrument of torture (as still in the English travail—and also travel!). If scholē means leisure, rest, ease, ascholia means to be busy (nervous due to lack of time), occupation, business.

165. ". . . tolle tempus, occidens est oriens" (eliminate time, and evening is morning—or west is east), as Meister Eckhart so pregnantly puts it; *Exposition Sancti Evangelii sec. Iohannem,* Nr. 8 (L.W. III, 9).

166. Cf. my Hindu–Christian essay in this regard, "The Myth of Prajāpati. The Originating Fault or Creative Immolation," in Panikkar, *Myth, Faith and Hermeneutics,* op. cit.

167. "Sed quia Deus uno actu et se et omnia intelligit, unicum Verbum eius est expressivum non solum Patris, sed etiam creaturam." St. Thomas, *Sum. Theol.* I, q.34, a.1.

168. Cf. the *hodie,* the *today* of the Easter liturgy in the Christian rite. Today the world is redeemed, because today it is created and today risen again.

169. Cf. L. Silburn, *Instant et cause. Le discontinu dans la pensée philosophique de l'Inde,* Paris (Vrin) 1955. Silburn remarks that there has been a general incomprehension regarding this fundamental Buddhist tenet.

170. Cf. R. Panikkar, "Time and History in the Tradition of India: kāla and karma," UNESCO *Cultures and Time,* Paris (The UNESCO Press) 1976, pp. 63–88.

171. Cf. Luke I, 25–32. He saw in Jesus Christ the fullness of time.

172. Cf. Luke XXIII, 43.

173. Cf. the astonishing injunction of the Gospel: not to worry about the morrow, or be concerned, or remember ("me merimnate" [25]), Matthew VI, 19–34. Cf. the same "amerimnos" (free from care—without memory, and without divided being) of I Cor. VII, 32. Cf. Phil. IV, 6.

174. The great temptation of all religions is to cut the constitutive tension

between the *ex* and the *sistence,* the temporal and the eternal, the *vyāvahārika* and the *paramārthika,* the *samsāra* and the *nirvāṇa,* the earthly and the heavenly, appearance and reality, the phenomenon and the noumenon, the bad and the good, the tares and the wheat, the secular and the sacred, etc.

175. Although the phenomenon is not reducible to the so-called "New Religions," they offer a good example. Cf. J. Needleman and G. Baker (eds.), *Understanding the New Religions,* New York (Seabury) 1978 for an exclusively North American approach. Cf. also G. Lanczkowski *Die neuen Religionen,* Frankfurt a.M. (Fischer) 1974, for a world panorama and the previous studies by G. Guariglia, V. Lanternari, and E. Benz.

176. Cf. the words of Milan Kundera, the exiled Czech writer living in Paris, as reported by the *Christian Science Monitor* (29 July 1981, p. B2): "The small nations of central Europe have never pretended to make history. They have always been its victims. Hegel and his cult of history could never have been a Czech or a Hungarian. Kafka could never have been a Russian."

177. "The scheme through which industrial society churns out its past has been called history," says Ivan Illich in his polemical style, *Vernacular Gender,* Cuernavaca, *Tecno-politica,* Doc. 07.81, p. 58.

178. Cf. R. Panikkar, *Das Heil der Welt (pro manuscripto);* e.g., *Bhagavad Gītā* III, 32; IV, 40; VII, 3, 19; IX, 3; XII, 5; etc.

179. This has been the persistent belief of humankind throughout the ages, following the cosmological paradigm that only a tiny little portion of any given plane reaches the higher one: more water than earth and more earth than plants: these are more numerous than animals and animals outnumber Men. So the elect are also fewer in number. To reach a higher birth or total release is a privilege, perhaps a calling, and thus a duty—but not a right, certainly not a birthright; it would have to be a re-birth-right.

180. Cf. K. Rahner, *Zur Theologie der Zukunft,* München (DTV) 1971.

181. "Comment lui assigner un but? (à l'histoire) Si elle en avait un, elle ne l'atteindrait qu'une fois parvenue à son terme.", writes E. M. Ciovan in *Écartèlement,* op. cit., p. 42. He also refers to ". . . ce défi à la contemplation qu'est l'histoire." (60)

182. Here are the causes for the flourishing of so many "New Religions" and sects promising to deliver the goods for their members here and now. And here also are the dangers of confusing transhistorical consciousness with the desire for instantaneous gratification, pleasure, well-being—and thus the role of drugs.

183. Cf. the traditional Hindu homologation (since the *Śatapatha Brāhmana,* vg. VI, 1, 1, 1–15; VI, 1, 1, 2, 1–13; XI, 1, 6, 1–11) between the four types of beings created by Brahmā and the four times of the world (and thus of the day): Dawn is the time of Men; Daylight is the time of the Gods; Evening twilight the time of the Fathers (ancestors, *pitṛs*); and Night the time of the De-

mons. Man's life is intertwined with these four dimensions of Time, the highest God, according to the *Atharva Veda*, XIX, 53–54.

184. Fate is from the Latin *fatum*, p.p. of *fari*, to speak; thus the past participle means the spoken, i.e. the definitive sentence spoken by the Gods; but also with the connotations of *fame* and *fable*, which open up room for freedom.

185. From the Latin *dēstināre*, to determine, arrange, make firm, establish; from *de-stanāre*, to settle, fix; from *stāre*, to stand. (Cf. Sanskirt *sthānam*, place, stand.) Cf. also Novalis' phrase describing the true historian as the "Liebhaber des Schicksals." (*Schriften*, J. Minor [ed.], 1932, II, p. 315, Apud Scholtz, *art. cit.*)

186. From the Old English *hlot:* portion, choice and also decision (German *Los*); an object used to assign more or less by chance, casting lots for a reward, a duty, etc. (Cf. lottery, to allot, etc.) In ancient German, it conserved the meaning of "Opferanteil der Götter, Opferblut" and, of course, "Erbschaft," inheritance. Cf. Latin *clavis*, key; *claudere*, to close; etc. Not etymologically but semantically connected with *moira* (the Greek Destiny), with the original meaning of "lot, portion." The verb *meíromai* means to participate. Cf. *méros* = part, portion; *merízo*, to divide. Cf. the Latin *mereo* = I merit, in the sense that I gain, i.e. gain a portion, merit a part (of the profit of the work or action).

187. Cf. the Spanish Constitution of the IInd Republic (of 1931): "España es una república de trabajadores de todas clases." Cf. the Marxist ideology: In the USSR, it is illegal not to work.

188. Cf. my *Colligite Fragmenta*, op. cit.

189. The name of Nietzsche, with his ambivalent attack on history, should be mentioned here.

190. I have to insist that these three words are used here as codes for the trends described, and are in no way directly linked with Buddhism, or Christianity, or Hinduism. My reflection here is a cross-cultural one, not a comparative enterprise.

191. The common observation of Westerners coming to India that the population is selfish and insensitive to the issues of common comfort, work and civilization, stems from the fact that all these concerns are not ultimately taken seriously. It is all played by ear, according to circumstances, without any of the convictions of the Western type of work-ethic.

192. The seriousness of the Latin American "Theology of Liberation" has often been misunderstood in traditional Christian circles as mere social work or a dilution of the transcendent nature of the Christian Kingdom of God. It all depends on whether this Kingdom is already there, or is to be expected, or built in collaboration between Man and God—i.e., whether salvation is interpreted as *nirvāna* or *sotēría*. Gandhi's *satyagraha* for a Rāmraj (a divine kingdom) also goes in the same direction.

SUMMARY OF RESPONSE AND DISCUSSION

Dr. Huston Smith followed by telling of a recent conversation with Dr. Ewert Cousins wherein he had expressed several reservations concerning Teilhard. The first reservation concerned Teilhard's claim that *The Phenomenon of Man* is a work of science. The second concerned any attempt to ground theology in science, for the science of today will one day be out of date. Thirdly, the crux of science is the controlled experiment. Since we can control only what is inferior to ourselves, a superior intelligence would not show up in a scientific view-finder. Fourth, to speak of God as final Cause of evolution is to introduce purpose and this violates the canons of science. Cousins answered,

> Just as Dante used the Ptolemaic cosmology of his day as symbolic framework for *The Divine Comedy,* so Teilhard uses the cosmology of our time to frame his vision. In both cases the vision exceeds the cosmology and is not endangered should the cosmology be superseded.

Smith concluded,

> I could hear that, and it helped me as I turned back to Teilhard in anticipation of this conference. If we do not read him like fundamentalists, as if he were writing literal science, but instead read his "science" allegorically and symbolically, we can see how his writings have healing power. This conference testifies to that power.

Prigogine objected to Panikkar's concept of a pretemporal human phase, for temporality seems to have characterized man as far back as we can trace. Furthermore, the scientific world does acknowledge eternity.

> We have a truth which is not changing in a changing environment. We find ourselves somewhere between motion and eter-

nity. This somewhere has to be defined. . . . But I do not think it does justice to the complexity of the problem to speak of a new nontemporal period.

Prigogine also objected to Smith's claim that science deals only with what it can control. He saw this attitude characterizing Newtonian science but not the science of the present day.

8

Summary of Final Discussion

The final session of the Symposium involved all six speakers on the stage with Father Burghardt as moderator. Among themselves they had identified three themes that seemed profitable to discuss:

1. How does science, specifically modern science, contribute to the unity of knowledge?
2. How does history or historical consciousness contribute to the unity of knowledge?
3. How does Teilhard's own vision contribute to the unity of knowledge?

Dr. Prigogine was invited to open the discussion by addressing the first question. He began by observing that science looks different to those outside the scientific community and those within. From the outside science seems to proceed by a kind of logic in a peaceful and automatic way; but from the inside there is a lot of trial and error and nobody knows how it will turn out. He saw Newtonian science introducing "the combination of science-as-theoretical-concept and science-as-praxis." This combination meant that there is a path of communication between the soul and the material world. Nature itself was seen as "subject to eternal and unchanging laws which could in principle always be predicted," but the scientist himself was outside of the world that was being described. In contemporary science this is no longer true: "the observer is involved in what he describes." Thus science and other human activities are converging today, and of this convergence Teilhard was acutely aware.

Panikkar objected that science has a meaning within each culture and to extrapolate this meaning to another culture is not always possible. Prigogine responded, "I would not say that present day science is an expression of Western civilization and is culturally bound. If correctly understood, it is much less culturally bound than we used to think." Panikkar responded, "The present day status of science implies a conception of matter, world, energy, force and time which is very peculiar to one group of civilizations and is not universal." Prigogine answered that, "One cannot speak of a monolithic construct of science and associate it with Western civilization; science has grown in many directions." As "Modern art" is a construct that includes many different approaches, so modern science does not have a unified point of view on time, energy and matter.

Leakey spoke up for the trans-cultural character of science: "Scientific facts are convertable currency; they cross all ideological barriers." Science is to determine the facts and the rules that govern them; the application of these facts is another matter and this application is seldom the job of the scientist. Panikkar still had reservations: just as there is no tool without a user (a tool without a user is not a tool), so "there is no scientific fact without a mind which considers it a scientific fact."

Soleri presented an unfamiliar understanding of technology, but one much in the spirit of Teilhard. Since evolution is a building process that has been going on throughout the millennia, technology has antedated humanity. But with the coming of humanity, "technology became conscious of itself." Seen in this light, science is the human effort to understand the cosmos in order to give new instruments to the technological process in which it is already engaged. The role of religion is to define an ideal perfection, and the role of science is to show the way to reach that perfection.

Boulding pointed out an assumption involved in even speaking of the unity of knowledge, that is that the world is unified. "The real world may consist of a lot of incompatible systems, and it may have different systems at different times." He said that he was more interested in the truth of our knowledge than in its unity. He defined truth in terms of a one-to-one mapping between the thoughts in our mind and the structures of the real world. We can recognize our errors when they do not stand up to the test: "an error is a little less stable than the truth." Prigogine developed the thought of Boulding by speaking of science permitting a dialogue between man and nature. We can imagine things and then we test what we have imagined. He quoted Einstein to the effect that we question nature and nature generally says, No; but occasionally it says, Perhaps. Prigogine was pressed to say how science as dialogue with nature differs with other dialogues with nature. He answered science was less difficult to communicate to others.

Mr. Leakey was asked to introduce the second question: what historical consciousness contributes to the unity of knowledge. He saw science developing out of a western point of view and against the frame-work of time as written and documented in history. The Europeans looked down on the Africans because they did not have a written history. But the Africans had a history and a philosophy that was oral. And ancient peoples have left magnificent works of art:

> I think the beginning of historical consciousness is open to discussion. Burial ceremonies in human societies took place before the written word. The earliest known burials date from around 70,000 B.C. If you take art to its earliest form, you would find abstract art going back as far as 300,000 years ago.

In each case Leakey saw the human mind involved with activities that are not simply functional.

Panikkar spoke of historical consciousness as a myth. He defined a myth as "something you believe in without believing you believe in it." It is like speaking with an accent; one is not aware of it oneself—but those who speak differently are aware of it. The West lives by a myth according to which things are real only when they can be localized in time and space; in the same way the fulfillment of one's life is expected in time.

Prigogine took exception to Panikkar's presentation of time in the West. He quoted Einstein as saying, "For us convinced physicists, we know that time is an illusion." Prigogine did not want to allow that time was either everything or nothing at all. He related the issue to the theme, the Unity of Knowledge:

> If there would be one type of knowledge accessible to us which would be nontemporal and another type of knowledge which would be temporal, then there would be a basic dichotomy. Therefore, perhaps the main question is, are there two

types of knowledge, or is there only one type of knowledge which is essentially temporal?

Boulding saw "historical consciousness" as the image we have in our mind of the past and future. The image of the past is increasing as we learn more and more about the past. Copleston developed this understanding of the past by saying that we are being set free of the past, for we realize that the past exists only in the reconstructions of the historians: "as reflection sets in, we seem to be set free from the weight of the past and historic consciousness."

Father Copleston was then asked to introduce the final question: what does Teilhard contribute to the unity of knowledge? Copleston saw Teilhard presenting an ideal term of the universe: "the total convergence of the universe in relation to each part of itself." He made a comparison with Hegel:

> In Hegelian terms one could speak of reality coming to self-reflection or to knowledge of itself in and through the human mind. I take it that that was Teilhard's ideal.

Soleri saw this convergence in the increasing sensitization of the cosmos to itself. This involves a "slow consummation of the parameters of time, space and mass energy into what Teilhard has anticipated as the Omega Point."

Panikkar indicated that there are some cultures that do not accept the belief that there is a single Being, Mind or God for whom oneness will be final. They would not allow the unified universe described by St. Paul wherein ultimately God will be all in all. "I think the greatness of Teilhard is that he spelled out for us this latent tendency towards unity."

Leakey expressed a general difficulty with the conversation. He said he knew of only a single reality: "The fact that I am holding a pen is real and the fact that it will drop if I let it go is real." Thus, the unity of knowledge means showing how the systems of the world work and how we can manage them:

> I think the unity of knowledge as Teilhard saw it was an attempt to understand in an incontrovertible way what this world is and how we are part of it. Because on such a basis we

can define systems wherein we can coexist in love and peace. .... I think that what Teilhard was trying to say was that those who believe strongly in the importance of the spiritual world can reconcile their understandings with someone who believes simply in the physical world and sees life within it. And indeed I am one of the latter.

Several speakers told of the reality of the spiritual world. Then Prigogine related his talk more closely to Teilhard:

During my lecture . . . I described the chemical clock in which there are millions and millions of independent molecules manifesting a form of coherent behavior. In reading Teilhard I have the impression that he had a model of this type in mind. In such a model the size of the system is increasing and at the same time there are coherent interactions of independent units. When you go from monocellular to multicellular beings, some of the cells do behave in the same way as others, so subdivisions are defined. But in such an interacting dynamic system, the cells are not necessarily repressed. Rather, it forms a kind of nonrepressive ecological system in which there is a nonimposed diversity. And my impression is that for Teilhard unity included this kind of diversity and a tendency to build larger and larger systems towards planetization. The question is: can we have this diversity in larger and larger systems building to some ultimate unity? I think this question is the main challenge of the modern world.

Boulding followed with a personal appreciation of Teilhard: He said that he had been asking himself why he had resonated so deeply to *The Phenomenon of Man*. Then he told of finding there a sense of anguish that is brought on by science and the concept of evolution. He saw this anguish in Tennyson's *In Memoriam* and saw it involved with the realization of death.

Why was Teilhard a Christian? Was it not because there was something that had happened that had changed the world? Like the Michelson–Morley experiment had changed the world. After the Michelson–Morley experiment, science would never be the same again. The early Christians felt as if they had had a Michelson–Morley experiment. What had excited them was the claim that somebody had risen from the dead. That is what this meeting is all about. This is the scandal of Christianity; it is not philosophy at all. For the apostle Thomas it was something he touched. That is the only thing that people believe. Nobody believes eyes and ears. You see, that is what this University is all about. It is not philosophy; it is something far beyond that. And I think that what I sensed in Teilhard was this reconciliation. And Tennyson has the same thing too in the last verse of *In Memoriam*.

> The one far off divine event
> To which the whole creation moves.

That is Omega, is it not? I think the thing that I got out of Teilhard is the restoration of the poem of creation.

9

A Sermon for Teilhard's
Mass on the World

Thomas M. King, S.J.

At 10:45 on Sunday morning the participants gathered in the University Chapel for a Mass that began and ended with readings from Teilhard's Mass on the World. It included music by the Dahlgren Chapel Choir and dances by Betsy Beckman. The scriptural readings were chosen because they were favorites of Teilhard: Romans VIII, 19–23 tells of creation groaning together and hoping to escape its bondage to decay; Matthew XIV, 22–33 tells of Peter walking to Jesus over the water. Father Thomas King, S.J. gave the following homily.

I did not sleep much last night. There were too many things on my mind. I sat by my window and watched daylight spread over the Georgetown campus. Soon a bird began to sing and then there were many birds. It was much later that I heard the first human sounds. When the red sun finally rose over the Potomac I sensed thousands of eyes opening and responding to the light. Birds and humans, insects and beasts recommenced their daily labor. This evening, when the Symposium is over and the sun begins to sink behind the dark hills, many eyes that watched it rise will not still live to watch it set. St. Paul tells of all creation groaning together in its bondage to decay.

A bondage to decay. Long before we came here for this Symposium weekend, others came to the Georgetown campus and watched the sun rise and set—but the time came when they could watch no longer. But even before there were human eyes, strange mammal and reptile eyes watched the red sun rise over forests of hemlock that covered the wide floor of the Potomac Valley. And long before that this spot was part of the ocean floor and sea monsters glided in the red light of morning. Millennia of fossils have been deposited along the river's edge and tell of the immense bondage to decay, and of that bondage we are the present manifestation. But St. Paul spoke of the bondage as "not without hope."

Delaware and Piscataway Indians once gathered on this hillside and with the setting of the sun they told stories of birth and death. And in the telling they found their spirits reaching beyond themselves into the immense distances of the stars. An awesome summons seemed to draw them beyond the stories of mortality, so they spoke of immortal gods and circled around the ritual fire. Today we gather in their place; the chapel is brightly lit, but in terms of stellar distances our little lights do not reach much further than the lights of their fires.

Again we tell stories of birth and death and gather for a religious rite—and why? Because beyond the immense evidence of death an awesome spirit seems to assure the living, "It is I, do not be afraid." Perhaps our next step will be a difficult one, but perhaps like Peter in today's Gospel we have had the courage to answer, "Lord, if it is you, bid me to come to you walking on the water." How could Peter ever say that? How could he leave the safety of the boat? How can any of us do the same? Yet we do. The journey that all of us are called to make is a journey of faith, one that involves passing beyond the safety of what we are. But such a passage has always been at the heart of life: if life had not reached beyond itself, we would never have come to be. Today we hesitate as we see the wind and water. Yet if we do not believe, or if our faith falters, we will one day stand before the Divine Master and confronted with our own bungled lives will hear him say, "O ye of little faith, why have you doubted?"

Among you who have come to this Symposium there are probably many who have only begun to read Teilhard, and there are probably others who know him quite well. But I think there are two things about him that everyone in this Chapel knows: we know that he walked by faith and we know that his night was dark. Maybe your own night has been dark and the journey long; and that might be the reason that you have come to celebrate Teilhard. Perhaps there was a time when the testimony of his faith enabled you to press forward. And the mysterious journey of faith could resume, because for one brief moment you sensed you were not the only one there. I am here because the words of Teilhard enabled me to see that my own hesitant steps are not mine alone, but part of the immense journey of life itself pressing forward through the ages. The words of Teilhard have let me see that my own hesitant prayer, heavy with the bondage to decay, is part of the immense groaning together of all the living: 'Save us, Lord, lest we perish.' Let that prayer of Peter's be your own prayer as we continue this Mass. It is the prayer of all creation crying out to God with an immense hunger for life. And with the immense tenderness of Jesus may God bestow immortal food. Supporting one another let us advance over the dark water.

10

Concluding Remarks

Monika K. Hellwig

To end the Symposium, Fr. Burghardt, its remarkable moderator, called upon Dr. Hellwig to give a final reflection.

We gathered here to honor the memory and keep alive the heritage of Pierre Teilhard de Chardin. To that end we have been engaged in a living experiment in the unity of knowledge, and an exciting experiment it has been. It is my pleasant task to reflect on that experiment and to point to some of the highlights.

We began with a powerful vision laid before us. What I particularly appreciated in Father Copleston's talk was the permission, coming from a careful and exigent philosopher, to take some freedom to create, to dream, to make mistakes and to be a little crazy sometimes. One does not, after all, do much that is worthwhile without such permission. I also appreciated the plea for a philosophy of content as well as method, and the inclusion of theologians and other religious people in the common conversation. With philosophy in our days focussing more and more on method and less and less on content, we in theology sometimes have difficulty getting a hearing in that very sphere in which we should best participate, namely the philosophical discussion of human knowledge.

Similarly I appreciated Father Copleston's thesis about the dialectic of analysis and synthesis, for our society seems to be at a phase wherein analysis appears as the sophisticated operation and synthesis appears as the work of fools. It is a splendid thing that the speakers at this conference have not felt afraid to present their thought synthetically, that they have not been afraid to venture a little into one another's fields, to talk across barriers and venture some grand visions. Father Copleston so rightly defended Teilhard on the grounds that it is the grand vision and whether it answers problems and resolves tensions that decides whether a philosophy lives. Too often both philosophers and theologians do what appears to be the sophisticated thing, and it inspires no one because it does not carry over to a vision that motivates life.

Such work may be necessary. It is not sufficient, for we do not live by bread alone. We also live by the call to be, the call to be *for* something, for *someone,* for the Ultimate. Fittingly, therefore, Teilhard emerged in Father Copleston's talk as a paradigm for our present situation as scholars, as people dealing with ideas. Indeed, his life emerged as a parable because while his scientific work took him into studies increasingly specialized and esoteric, he felt a desperate need to speak to everyone and for everyone, a need to be in communion.

In that context it was a thrilling experience to see the scientist at work, in Professor Prigogine's talk, in a stance of great intellectual humility, a stance that takes its vantage point between the mastery of knowledge and the mysticism of self-surrender in communion. What moved me most was the final question: what is chaos and what is order? This suggests to us that either we might look at what science presents to us today with a panic-stricken sense of instability, or we might look at the same world with a sense of the exuberance of life and ask how and by whom that life is called forth and to what it tends.

In Dr. Leakey's presentation I greatly appreciated the focus on retrieving the lost evidence—the focus on not letting go of those aspects of experience that might be discarded because they do not last as artifacts or as literary traditions. It has much to do with the unity of knowledge to recognize that bias by which the paleontologist tries to read the whole life of a people from the stones and bones that remain. The question that I retain from Dr. Leakey's presentation is: what is part of any reality and what is its whole?

In Professor Boulding's delightful and inspirational talk I found two thoughts particularly significant for our discussion, namely his reflections on the relation of religion and science in general and his emphasis on Christian faith as legitimating science. I think this latter so well explains Teilhard; his Christian faith gave such radical coherence to what he was doing in science that it liberated him for his creative vision.

Quite different dimensions of the unity of knowledge were introduced by Father Panikkar and by Mr. Soleri. Quite apart from the contributions which their particular presentations made, they represented a challenge in their very persons. It is perhaps not accidental that most of the debate that took place over conflicting viewpoints involved Father Panikkar and his thesis about historical consciousness. In his person Father Panikkar represents the challenge to intercultural unity of knowledge. Similarly Mr. Soleri presents in this gathering the challenge to the unity of knowledge when it is explored and expressed in media other than words. He also presents a challenge for critical evaluation when he attempts to concretize the vision of Teilhard in architecture and city planning.

It seems particularly appropriate that our final session ended with a question about the connection between Teilhard's vision and the unity of knowledge. When we ask what it was that gave a focus to all knowledge for Teilhard himself, we must remember first of all that for him it was a hard won focus. His retrospective reflection, which most of you have probably read, tells us that he came by his focus with a great struggle, and suggests that his life was guided by two stars. One star was the trustworthiness, solidity, fidelity and conforting quality of matter which he could approach by scientific inquiry. The other was the trustworthiness, solidity, fidelity and comforting quality of the divine call in his life which he could pursue by religion. His own testimony, so moving for us, is that he first experienced the duality not as complementarity but as bitter conflict.

To resolve that conflict Teilhard went to the heart of Christian faith with the concept he named Christo-genesis, drawn from his traditional Catholic understanding of Incarnation. Indeed it follows quite coherently from his traditional Trinitarian faith, in which the God of creation, summoning all things into existence, summoning all things to himself, is not at all contradicted by the God revealed by Jesus at the center of history anticipating the end–time, and certainly to be known intimately by the continuing Christo-genesis.

This is what provides the focus for Teilhard. If there is truly an ultimate unifying call drawing all things into harmony in creation, in human freedom and activity, and in society, then of course there cannot ultimately be a conflict between what we discover in science and what we know by faith. Nor can there ultimately be a conflict among the various sciences which are simply various ways of knowing, ways of approaching reality. There cannot ultimately be a conflict between the knowing of the east and of the west, the knowing of the south and the north, nor even of the knowing of men and the knowing of women. In Teilhard's vision there must ultimately be complementarity but this is not established fact; it is a confident hope founded in faith.

What does this mean for us? For those of us who share Teilhard's faith it is a beacon light showing a way of harmonizing our own lives. For those who do not share his particular faith it leaves the very important question: what is that central point, understanding, inspiration in your life which gives the key to ultimate harmony? One cannot read Teilhard without being rather sternly challenged to answer that question.

An Afterword

During the final years of his life Teilhard had wanted to arrange a symposium that would involve many disciplines. But he expressed reservations about inviting "humanists," for frequently they do not see man in his context: they "make of man a world apart." But he would tell of similar reservations with many scientists: they leave the human observer outside of the objective world that they study. For Teilhard, man can be understood only through the universe and the universe understood only through man. They have developed together, and apart from each other they are mutually unintelligible. But through a unified comprehension of the cosmos known and man the knower Teilhard believed that one would become aware of a vast cosmic movement that reaches its completion in God. The unity of knowledge is not simply an objective ideal; it is also the foundation upon which people will come together and discover a common sense for God.

Perhaps this is what we found in the present Symposium. Speakers who had been formed by widely different systems of knowledge tried to understand each other and see in a different way. There were lively interchanges between speakers and members of the audience and people began to sense the common spirit of which Teilhard spoke; the Symposium seemed to have a life of its own. As participants left the auditorium on Sunday afternoon and walked out into the bright sunlight, many were reflecting on the final question asked by Dr. Hellwig: What is the central point or inspiration in your life that is the key to harmony? We knew what it was for Teilhard, and, because of the events in which we had shared, it had become a living question.

APPENDIX

Teilhard and Piltdown*

Thomas M. King, S.J.

Much of the following account is based on a lecture by Dr. J. S. Weiner delivered at Georgetown University, April 28, 1981. Weiner—together with Kenneth Oakley and W. E. LeGros Clark—uncovered the Piltdown hoax in 1953. Weiner immediately began an extensive investigation to determine who was responsible. His account was published as The Piltdown Forgery *(Oxford, 1955; recently reissued as a Dover paperback). A videotape of Weiner's talk is available in the Georgetown University Library.*

In December 1912 newspapers around the world announced that the skull and jawbone of an early hominid had been found in the gravel beds of Piltdown, a quiet English village about forty-five miles south of London. From the same gravel beds came what appeared to be ancient tools together with hippo and elephant teeth. Soon a second site two miles distant was said to yield an ancient molar and fragments of a second skull. Anthropologists generally accepted the finds. But as additional human fossils were found in Asia and Africa, Piltdown became a puzzling anomaly. Then in November 1953 it was announced that the fossils were part of an elaborately contrived forgery. The skull was human and somewhat recent, while the jawbone had come from an orang-utan. Both had been stained and doctored to appear as part of a single ancient hominid. In 1953, before the public story broke, Weiner went to

Piltdown and began gathering information on the supposed finders. His attention soon focused on Charles Dawson, an amateur collector of some standing who was at the center of all the events. In 1955 Weiner published his carefully documented case against Dawson. Teilhard is mentioned several times in Weiner's account, for as a seminarian he had been with Dawson at Piltdown. Since Stephen Gould allows that "J. S. Weiner's elegant case virtually precludes Dawson's innocence," the only question considered here is whether Teilhard assisted Dawson in preparing the forgery—as Gould has charged.

Now to the major points of Gould's accusation:

First Point: Errors in Teilhard's letters to Oakley shortly after the hoax was exposed. Teilhard was seventy-two and working at what is now the Wenner Gren Foundation for Anthropological Research in New York when a front-page story in the *New York Times* (Nov. 22, 1953) announced the elaborate hoax. Kenneth Oakley wrote Teilhard asking him for his recollections of Piltdown. Teilhard's response included an account of how Dawson

> brought me to the site of Locality 2 and explained me (sic) that he had found the isolated molar and the small pieces of skull in the heaps of rubble and pebbles raked at the surface of the field.

Oakley had difficulty with this part of Teilhard's account, so he wrote back saying that he was very unsure when the skull fragments and tooth were found. He asked Teilhard whether this visit to the second site was before or after the supposed discovery. Teilhard responded that Oakley's question had made him doubt. But then he concluded:

> Yes, I think definitely they *had* been already found; and that is the reason why Dawson pointed to me the little heaps of raked pebbles at the site of the "discovery."

Having recounted this, Gould states his case:

> Dawson "discovered" the skull bones at Piltdown 2 in January 1915, and the tooth not until July 1915. And now, the key point: Teilhard was mustered into the French army in December 1914 and was shipped immediately to the front, where he

remained until the war ended. He could not have seen the remains of Piltdown 2 with Dawson unless they had manufactured them together before he left (Dawson died in 1916).

Gould presents this "slip" of Teilhard as his central evidence. But in stating his case Gould has significantly altered what Teilhard said. Teilhard has told of seeing the *site,* but in writing of this Gould has Teilhard seeing "the *remains* of Piltdown 2." Gould goes on to write as though Teilhard had claimed to have "actually viewed the fossils," the "finds," the "material," "seen the specimens." The difference between seeing the site and seeing the fossils is significant. If Teilhard had seen the fossils he would have studied them with care and his memory of them would have been more vivid. But that is not all: There is a letter from Dawson to Smith Woodward of the British Museum dated July 3, 1913 in which Dawson tells of finding "the frontal part of a human skull" at another site, "a plough field a long way from Piltdown." (Weiner brought a copy of this important letter with him to Georgetown.) Thus, finds did not begin at Location 2 (as Teilhard quite understandably thought the new site to be) in January 1915—as Gould has claimed—but *in July 1913.* In August of 1913 Dawson and Teilhard traveled about the whole area, and Dawson showed Teilhard this second site. In doing so he probably would have indicated the rubble wherein he had recently claimed to have found a piece of skull. Then the whole basis of Gould's charge would reduce to this: Dawson showed Teilhard the heaps of rubble wherein he claimed to have found a piece of skull. Forty years later Teilhard recalled the event but misstated the extent of Dawson's claim.

Apart from this error Gould insists that Teilhard's letters to Oakley are "filled with other damaging points," "a series of slips and halftruths." Three are identified: *First,* in a letter to his family dated May 1909 Teilhard told of meeting Dawson. But in writing to Oakley in 1954 he dated this meeting as 1911. Teilhard's error is undeniable; Gould sees it as an attempt to divert suspicion from himself. *Second,* When Oakley asked Teilhard about something Dawson had done in 1908, Teilhard responded, "In 1908 I did not know Dawson." Gould allows that this is true. But because Teilhard did not spontaneously add that he met Dawson in the early months of 1909 he includes this in his list of slips and half truths! *Third,* Teilhard's letters to his family tell of many travels about the countryside: but when he wrote to Oakley he told of being largely confined to his seminary room. The author of the present article was in a Jesuit seminary in the 1950s and recalls being confined to a seminary room to an extent that modern readers would not believe. My letters home at this time tell of bicycle rides about the countryside as this was the only other thing I did. Gould speculates about Teilhard and Dawson spending "long hours in field and pub;" in this Gould shows little familiarity with seminary life before Vatican II.

Gould insists that there is a pattern of misstatements in Teilhard's letters to Oakley and that the pattern shows Teilhard trying to excuse himself. But when Gould's evidence is correctly stated it seems that Teilhard made two errors in recalling events forty years before: (1) When Dawson showed him the rubble at the second site Dawson had probably claimed only a piece of skull (not pieces of skull and a molar) had been found there. (2) Teilhard met Dawson in 1909 and not in 1911.

> *Note:* Teilhard erred in stating a date. But one could note that Gould has three erroneous dates in stating his charge: Teilhard entered the Jesuits in1899 (not 1902): he was ordained in 1911 (not 1912); his Parisian letters continued till 1914 (not 1912). So it goes. Gould's effective style can be perplexing: in the same paragraph as he tells of Teilhard's letters to Oakley trying "to exonerate Dawson," he tells of Teilhard in the same letters trying "to extricate himself alone." These letters can be consulted in their entirety; they are published in *Teilhard de Chardin: L'oeuvre scientifique,* p.4561 ff. In these letters Teilhard is reluctant to see Dawson as dishonest. Gould would have it that he stonewalls. Weiner argues, "If he (Teilhard) had been guilty, he might have been ready to see Dawson accused and thus avert suspicion from himself. He did not take this view. He was bewildered." Gould sees Teilhard burdened with life-long guilt. It could be argued that if Teilhard did have such a burden of guilt he would have remembered each painful detail. If he felt any need to conceal complicity, he could easily have consulted the official accounts of Piltdown and thus avoid incriminating himself. It seems that he simply stated what he recalled and in the process made two small errors.

Second Point: Teilhard's one article on Piltdown was followed by virtual silence. Teilhard wrote only a single article on Piltdown—a popular article published in December 1920. In the twenty-three volumes of his collected works (apart from this article and a thirteen line paragraph) Teilhard made only passing references to Piltdown. His 1920 article claimed that the skull and jaw came from different individuals. This considerably diminished the importance of the find, but Teilhard went on to say that the skull itself had considerable significance. After this 1920 article, Teilhard made only minimal reference to Piltdown. Gould sees this of particular significance as he would see Piltdown supporting one of Teilhard's favorite ideas: multiple human lineages could argue for the domination of spirit over matter. But such arguments become difficult to manage; perhaps the large and ancient skull of Piltdown followed by later smaller skulls (as seemed to be the case) would argue for the domination of matter over spirit. That the twenty-three volumes make only occasional reference to Piltdown is neither extraordinary nor "silence to the point of perversity" (Gould). Ten of these volumes are scientific reprints detailing excavations that Teilhard was making in Asia. The others are religious and philosophical works that treat frequently of evolution. But more striking than their rare mention of Piltdown Man is their rare mention of Peking Man—an authentic fossil about which Teilhard centered his scientific career.

Weiner spoke with Teilhard in the summer of 1954 and asked him about his infrequent references to Piltdown. Telling of this conversation, Weiner explained:

> I had no reason then and I have no reason now—I have said so in public many times—to see in Teilhard a fellow conspirator. But I was interested in one point: I asked Teilhard why he had paid rather little attention to Piltdown after 1920. I wondered whether he had in fact suspected something and therefore began to write less and less about Piltdown, (whether he) might have had some inkling.

Teilhard said that he suspected nothing. He explained his silence by saying that he did not believe that the two parts had come from the same animal. He added that the events took place before he had much training and he had not seen all of the material. (Weiner retains a lingering doubt that perhaps Teilhard had suspected some irregularity, "but he never could take it on himself to denounce anybody. He did not have the evidence.")

Third Point: Other fossil teeth found with the Piltdown skull. Hippopotamus and elephant teeth were supposedly found near the doctored skull. It seems they were added to authenticate and date the find. Subsequently they have been traced to Malta and Tunisia. Gould uses the teeth to further implicate Teilhard as Teilhard had traveled from France to Egypt in 1905 and returned in 1908. Gould notes that the trip to Egypt did not pass these areas (it went by way of Messina and Crete). As for the return voyage in 1908 Gould writes an amazing sentence: "I can find no trace of his passage back, and the two areas (Malta and Tunisia) are right on his route from Cairo to France." Yes—Gould is able to identify Teilhard's return route in the same sentence in which he tells us he found no record. Malta and Tunisia were not on Teilhard's route down. Is there any reason to situate them on Teilhard's return route other than to implicate Teilhard? Gould allows that Dawson might have obtained the fossils elsewhere. But he does not tell us that Dawson had a stepson with the British army in the Sudan who had loaded Dawson's house with African souvenirs. Nor does he speculate on return routes from the Sudan passing through Malta and Tunisia.

I am well aware of the difficulties involved when an historian in 1980 tries to identify the source of fossil teeth for an incident in 1912. But there are significant texts concerning the teeth that date from the year of the forgery. Teilhard wrote to his parents on April 26, 1912:

> Last Saturday, my geologist friend, Mr. Dawson, came for a visit. He brought me some prehistoric remains (silex, elephant and hippopotamus teeth, and especially, a very thick well-preserved skull) which he had found in the alluvium deposits not far from here; he did this to stir me up to some similar expeditions, but I hardly have time for that anymore.

This seems to be the earliest reference to the teeth and to the skull-teeth-Dawson-Teilhard connection. The letter could give Gould several problems: Teilhard's letters to *cher papa* and *chere maman* are filled with tenderness and filial piety; then why is he making his mother and father the first victims of the Piltdown hoax? Further, Dawson had been showing the skull all around the neighborhood since the Spring of 1908 (before Teilhard had come to the area). If Dawson and Teilhard were three-year companions in natural history—as Gould would have it—why did he not show him the skull before this time?

Note: Previous letters of Teilhard to his parents tell of a first meeting with Dawson in May 1909, a single exchange of letters, a day of common exploration, and three visits of Dawson to the seminary (in the French edition these letters are numbered #18, 21, 23, 33, 39, 64). It is unlikely that they had any additional meetings during those three years. Gould would seem to overstate it in calling them three-year companions in natural history, or "good friends and colleagues," or "warm friends, colleagues and co-explorers." Weiner sees a different relationship. He told of the letters that Teilhard later wrote to Dawson as "unmistakably letters of a junior person writing to a senior man in great deference and respect." Teilhard's letters to his parents tell of his first visit to Dawson's home in June 1912. He left England for France on July 16 of that all important year. Gould with his general tendency to overstate Teilhard's involvement has Teilhard staying in England until "late in 1912." A curious circumlocution to indicate July 16!

Fourth Point: Teilhard's glum disinterest in viewing a London exhibit concerning the hoax. In August of 1954 while returning from Paris to New York, Teilhard stopped in London to see Oakley and others. Oakley found him reluctant to discuss Piltdown and Teilhard walked glumly past an exhibit showing how the hoax was uncovered. Gould interprets Teilhard's reaction as "intense embarrassment" and ascribes this embarrassment to guilt. Apart from this interpretation there seems to be some question of Teilhard's mood at the time. During the same visit to England Weiner spoke with Teilhard concerning Piltdown for about an hour. Weiner did not find Teilhard reluctant: "He (Teilhard) discussed all the points that I put to him perfectly frankly and openly." That Teilhard was glum at the time seems to be certain. Five days before coming to London he was in Paris when his religious superiors ordered him to terminate his visit, to leave Paris and not return. Teilhard saw this as the final rejection of the religious message of his life. Several days after receiving this order he was twice led past an exhibit showing how he had been duped. So he was glum!

Fifth Point: Other anthropologists suspected Teilhard. Gould does not list this as one of his points, but weight is added to his argument by telling of others who suspected Teilhard. Weiner commented on three of these: Louis Leakey, Kenneth Oakley and W. E. LeGros Clark. Leakey twice published his suspicions concerning Teilhard; this gave some currency to Teilhardian complicity before Gould took up the charge. Weiner commented: "I know that Louis Leakey felt that Teilhard had a hand in it. But I asked him about it and he had no evidence." (The official biographer of the Leakey family writes, "Louis had no real evidence, only a hunch.") Concerning Kenneth Oakley, Weiner stated:

> Gould would have you accept that Oakley was the same mind (as himself); but it is not so. When Gould's article came out Oakley dissociated himself from it. He wrote to the (London) *Times* pointing out that Teilhard's letters disturbed him; but since there was no positive evidence against Teilhard he should have the benefit of the doubt. But I have seen Oakley recently and he has no reservations—that I felt—about his belief that Teilhard had nothing to do with the planting of this material and manufacture of the fraud.

As to the opinion of W. E. LeGros Clark, Weiner states,

> I saw him practically every day from 1953 until after he retired in 1965. I never heard him controvert my opinion that Dawson had done it alone.

Apart from the major points listed by Gould his case would seem to contain additional errors: Gould would have it that Teilhard was the only one to find any of the material *in situ*. Weiner objects that "three or four things were definitely found *in situ*." Gould claimed that Teilhard and Dawson were companions in natural history for three years before any professionals saw the material. Weiner objected that several professionals had seen the material before Teilhard (Abbott, Woodhead, and others). Gould claims that Teilhard wrote eleven letters home telling of excursions with Dawson. Using the same collection of letters one finds that eleven letters mention Dawson, but only six tell of common excursions (several concern the same event).

After Gould has listed his evidence against Teilhard, he warns us that the evidence may be overwhelming, but we are still not satsified unless there is a reasonable motive. Here he sees "no great problem." He does not believe that Teilhard acted with malice or with hope of a reward. Instead he proposes that Teilhard became involved with Piltdown as a prank; it was a youthful caper. However events passed beyond his control to become "a joke that went too far." Why the prank? Gould conjectures that at the time Teilhard was only an amateur with no hope of a professional career in science. Furthermore, Teilhard was French; then why not play a delicious joke on the British professionals? But Gould observes, "the joke quickly went sour."

The recognized sequence of events conflicts with all of these conjectures: Teilhard's letters show that the joke had begun by April 1912, it continued through his finding a canine tooth in August of 1913, and included Teilhard's article of 1920 that still argued for the significance of Piltdown. How can eight years of active deceit be termed a joke that *quickly* went sour? As to the "joke:" Weiner sees too much careful preparation of the fossils for it to be only a joke. As for it being a youthful caper: Teilhard was thirty-nine in 1920. Second, if for some reason Teilhard did want to delude the British professionals (for which there is no evidence), why did he first delude his unsuspecting parents living in rural France? Third, Weiner asks, "Why should Teilhard wish to deceive Professor Smith Woodward, Sir Arthur Keith, and others who had been so kind to him?" Fourth, in the Spring of 1912 arrangements had been made for Teilhard to begin professional studies in geology. When the canine was found in August 1913 Teilhard had completed his first year of these with the master of French paleontology, Marcellin Boule. Gould ignores this to claim that at the time Teilhard had no hope of a professional career. Scientists do not take kindly to such jokes (and Jesuit superiors are much the same). Then why would Teilhard want to ruin his career as both scientist and priest to play a pointless joke on British professionals? By August of 1913 Piltdown had become the focus of an international search for human origins. If Teilhard had announced his "joke" at this time, would Marcellin Boule have received him back into his lab?

Note: Concerning motivations: Weiner has told of Dawson being long eager to be received into the Royal Society (of science). Gould seems to accept this as Dawson's motivation, while maintaining that Teilhard was pranking (June 1981). Gould explains that conspirators frequently have different motivations. This is probably true, but it does not apply here. How could they conspire if Teilhard were joking and Dawson were trying to gain admission to the Royal Society? A joke would require that the hoax be revealed to embarrass the British professionals; while Dawson's promotion would require that the hoax remain concealed.

It is clear that I find Gould's case altogether lacking in evidence, but ultimately my belief in Teilhard's innocence is based on his character. First, Teilhard was an honest man, as many of his associates have testified. Second, he was a shy man who was not given to practical jokes (Gould gives no evidence of other pranks). Third, Gould envisions Teilhard suffering guilt, remorse, galling bitterness almost beyond belief, and weeping inwardly as friends fall for a hoax that he is powerless to undo. These data-free conjectures ignore the incredible documentation available on the psyche of Teilhard: Apart from the twenty-three volumes mentioned above, Teilhard left about 8,000 personal letters and twenty-some copy books of a private journal. I have read the vast majority of these and find no support for the speculative psycho-history offered by Gould. Some theologians have criticized Teilhard as lacking a sense of sin and guilt. Now without offering a single reference, Gould has "no real problem" in turning him into a guilt tortured Kierkegaard.

In sum: Gould's case would seem to involve the following errors. Teilhard claimed to have seen only the site and not the remains or fossils of Piltdown 2. Dawson's first account of a second Piltdown site was in July 1913—not January 1915. Six associations in three years is hardly a three-year companionship: and six letters—not eleven—tell of common excursions. Testimonials by Oakley and LeGros Clark seem inaccurate. Several dates are in error and July 16 is hardly "late in 1912." Glum disinterest does not necessarily imply guilt. Several professionals saw Piltdown material before Teilhard. Diggers other than Teilhard found fossils *in situ*. A return route from Egypt and a psycho-history have been invented to fit.

Gould has done considerable exploration into a long-buried event, and out of a few splinters has created a new image of both Piltdown and Teilhard. But the world's expert on Piltdown (with no detectable interest in Teilhard's philosophy) is not at all convinced, and Teilhardian scholars do not recognize the image they are being offered. Vast amounts of material concerning Teilhard has been ignored, and Weiner tells of having boxes of material on Piltdown that Gould has not asked to consult. As one long familiar with the mind of Teilhard, I can only say what Teilhard said of Piltdown Man in 1920: anatomically the pieces do not fit.

NOTES

*"A Response to Stephen Jay Gould's Charge of Teilhard Complicity" (see *Natural History,* March 1979, Aug. 1980, June 1981).

PRINCIPAL CONTRIBUTORS

KENNETH BOULDING—Economist, educator and poet. He has served as president of the American Association for the Advancement of Science and of the American Economic Association. He serves on the advisory board of the Teilhard Foundation and is Distinguished Professor of Economics Emeritus from the University of Colorado. Among his many publications are *The Impact of the Social Sciences, Sonnets from the Interior Life, Redistribution through the Financial System,* and *Stable Peace and Ecodynamics.*

FREDERICK COPLESTON—Philosopher, Jesuit and Fellow of the British Academy. He is best known for *A History of Philosophy* in nine volumes and for his BBC debates with Bertrand Russell and A.J. Ayer. Recently he has given the Gifford Lectures and has published *Philosophies and Cultures* and *Religion and the One.* He sees Teilhard widening the scope of philosophy by presenting a distinctive world vision that synthesizes science, philosophy and religion.

RICHARD LEAKEY—Anthropologist and director of the National Museums of Kenya. Teilhard had a professional relationship with Richard's father, Louis Leakey, who spoke at a Teilhard Symposium in 1971. Like Teilhard Richard Leakey uses the evolutionary past to envision the possibility of human unity in the future. He relates this to the ethics of disarmament. Recently he has published *Origins, People of the Lake* and *The Making of Mankind;* these tell of finds of ancient man around Lake Turkana.

RAIMUNDO PANIKKAR—Professor of Comparative Religion at the University of California, priest of the diocese of Benares, India, and a member of the British Teilhard Association. He has doctorates in chemistry, philosophy and theology, and is author of twenty-nine books on the inter-relationships of world religions. Among these are *The Trinity and World Religions, The Vedic Experience* and *The Intra-Religious Dialogue.*

ILYA PRIGOGINE—Professor of Chemistry and Theoretical Physics at the University of Brussels and Director of the Center for Statistical Mechanics and Thermodynamics in Austin, Texas. Recipient of the Nobel Prize in chemistry in 1977 and an accomplished musician. Author of *From Being to Becoming* and *La Nouvelle Alliance;* the latter concerns the coming convergence of science and the humanities. His interest in Teilhard relates to his work in chemistry as well as his own optimistic understanding of the cosmos.

PAOLO SOLERI—Architect, philosopher and environmental planner. He came to the U.S. from Italy to study with Frank Lloyd Wright. For the past eleven years he has been building Arcosanti, a self-sufficient, one-building city for five thousand people stretching over fourteen acres of the Arizona desert. In September 1981 he dedicated a section of Arcosanti as the Teilhard Cloister. Soleri's writings include *Arcology, The Sketchbooks* and recently *Fragments.*

Additional Participants in the Symposium

IAN BARBOUR—Carleton College, author of *Issues in Science and Religion* and *Myths, Models and Paradigms.* Knew Teilhard when his father worked with him "in the field" in China. Responded to Frederick Copleston.

WALTER BURGHARDT—Patristic theologian and editor of *Theological Studies.* Recently published *Tell the Next Generation* and *Sir, We Would Like To See Jesus.* Moderator of the Symposium.

MONIKA HELLWIG—Georgetown University theologian known for her studies of the Church and the social meaning of the Gospel. Author of *Understanding Catholicism* and *Sign of Reconciliation and Conversion.* Responded to Kenneth Boulding and gave a final summary statement.

THOMAS KING—Georgetown University theologian. Author of *Teilhard's Mysticism of Knowing,* and *Sartre and the Sacred.* Jesuit priest and co-organizer of the Symposium.

JOHN O'KEEFE—Astronomer and geophysicist with the NASA Goddard Space Flight Center. Has worked on the geodesy of China and published two books on tektites. Responded to Ilya Prigogine.

DEAN PRICE—Georgetown University architect and winner of the National First Place Distinguished Design Award; has done research in energy systems. Heard Teilhard lecture in 1952. Responded to Paolo Soleri.

JAMES SALMON—Chemist and theologian from Loyola College, Baltimore. Co-author of a text, *Inorganic Chemistry.* Jesuit priest and co-organizer of the Symposium.

HUSTON SMITH—Syracuse University professor of both philosophy and religion. Became well known through a TV series on world religions and the book, *The Religions of Man;* recently published *Beyond the Post-Modern Mind.* Responded to Raimundo Panikkar.

J.S. WEINER—Uncovered the Piltdown hoax in 1953 and published *The Piltdown Forgery* in 1955. Has published abundantly on the adaptation to environment of human populations. Responded to Richard Leakey and prior to the Symposium defended Teilhard's limited Piltdown involvement as entirely innocent.